"Don't you hate it when..."

HOW TO SOLVE LIFE'S LITTLE IRRITATIONS

MARY ELLEN PINKHAM

"Don't you hate it when…"

HOW TO SOLVE LIFE'S LITTLE IRRITATIONS

BY MARY ELLEN PINKHAM

pinkham
PUBLISHING

Back cover photograph of Mary Ellen: Jim Arndt.
Book Design: Roy G Biv Creative 952.935.6565
For more of our products visit www.maryellenproducts.com

PINKHAM PUBLISHING PO BOX 39221, EDINA, MN 55439 218.327.9989

PRINTED IN THE UNITED STATES OF AMERICA First Printing: January 2005 ISBN 0-941298-13-2

Time magazine said, "She has probably contributed more to domestic felicity than Sara Lee. Nobel prizes have been awarded for less." *Ms.* magazine said, "The woman is fast becoming the technical adviser to the whole of American homemakery." They were talking about me.

The year was l980, and my new book, *Best of Helpful Hints*, had been on the best-seller list for months. **(Don't you hate it when someone brags about herself?)**

After so many years of telling folks how to clean their toilets, change the baby's diaper, and remove the pet accidents from the rug, I guess it's okay to give myself a pat on the back. I'm still amazed by my success, even though I always expected to be famous. Actually, I planned on being Miss America, but something got in my way. The competition. Still I bet I've had more fun than all the Miss Americas put together. **(Don't you hate it when people exaggerate?)**

I've certainly had a lot of satisfaction from what I do. Many people have told me how much my books have helped them, and I expect this one will, too. It's meant to help you deal with all kinds of everyday problems, and it's loaded with fun, fast and easy ideas. I've gathered them from experiences in my own home and garden; from the fans who shared them with me to include in my columns for the *Star* magazine, *Family Circle*, and *Woman's Day* and online at iVillage; and from researching my scripts and talking with the experts I've met in the course of shooting hundreds of episodes of HGTV's *TIPical Mary Ellen*. So they represent the best ideas that have come out of my 25 years of experience. **(Don't you hate it when time goes so fast?)**

I want to thank you for buying this book. I truly hope it makes your life easier.

Mary Ellen

This book is dedicated to my mother,
who always gave me good advice—like always moisturize
and wear sunscreen, or some day my skin would start to look old.
Of course, I didn't believe her.
(Don't you hate it when your mother turns out to be right?)

Contents

Don't you hate it when...
this happens?

I've used this symbol ✳ to highlight my favorite products, the ones that I find most useful and that really work. For your quick reference, you'll find the complete list (and buying information) at the end of the book.

Chapter 1
The Bathroom

Don't You Hate It When...

The shower track is really dirty

• A stiff paint brush, a toothbrush, or a grout brush are good tools for cleaning a shower track.

• To clean the shower door track thoroughly, the best solution is to remove the door. You will probably need a helper. Hold the door with one hand on each side, then lift it off the track.

The shower curtain is torn

• Repair torn shower curtain hole rings by applying strong, clear packaging tape to either side of the hole, and then make a new hole using a hole punch.

Don't you hate it when a fresh bouquet of roses flops over the next day?

• There are commercial kits available too.

• Or look for the new shower curtains that have slits on the top. They slip over the shower rods and there's no need for rings.

• You're less likely to get tears in the future if you spray ✳WD-40 along the rod.

The shower curtain attacks you

• Attach a small piece of Velcro to the hemmed side of the curtain and a companion piece to the wall of the shower or tub. You can purchase gizmos that do the same thing but they're expensive. (I read that one of Paul Newman's most annoying "don't-you-hate-it-whens" is having a shower curtain wrap around him. I wish he'd invite me over to fix it.)

Mold is growing on the bottom of a shower curtain

• Spray curtain with ✳Tilex with Bleach, let set and rinse off with hot water.

• Toss the shower curtain into the wash with a load of towels with chlorine or all-purpose bleach (whichever is appropriate for the towels).

The showerhead is clogged and stained

• Just use plain old vinegar and water to solve this problem. Simply put a chrome showerhead into a plastic bag filled with 1 part vinegar and 3 parts water, secure with a rubber band and let set overnight. In the morning, rinse. (Exception: This can't be used on any showerhead that has a

Don't you hate it when the only bathroom available is unisex?

Don't you hate it when you're waiting in line with a large container of fiber supplement and you run into your old boyfriend?

protective coating. If that's what you have, you should check with the manufacturer for the best cleaning method.)

A bathtub decal can't be budged

• If the tub is made of gelcoat or acrylic, cover the decal with aluminum foil and blow hot air on the foil with a hair dryer, lifting the edge. Slowly pull up and peel off the decal, trying to keep the top layer and clear adhesive together. If the layers do separate and the film tears as you go, lift the other edges around the decal and work toward the center until all of it is free. Remove the residue with ✴ WD-40 and use a plastic scraper or plastic credit card. If this doesn't work, call a professional.

• If the tub is porcelain enamel on cast iron or steel you can try the above, or spray with oven cleaner, wait 15 minutes and then scrape with a plastic scraper or an industrial safety razor.

• Or fold several layers of white paper towels over the decal and saturate the towels with mineral spirits or acetone (nail polish remover). Let stand for 15 minutes, then scrape. Caution: These chemicals are flammable. Keep the room well ventilated.

The bathroom drain is clogged

• Hair is usually the culprit. I have found that a long, thin, bendable brush works better than anything to remove hair from a drain. You can get them from Fuller Brush or purchase a ✶Hair Catching Brush. (The right size brush makes any cleaning job so much easier. Start a collection.)

• To prevent future clogging, stick a small piece of nylon netting into the tub or sink drain to catch the hairs.

• For tough jobs use a snake. (Home stores have snakes that can be rolled up. If you ever had one of the old-fashioned ones, you know what an improvement this is.)

Don't you hate it when you're invited over to watch someone else's home movies?

Grout is stained

• First, clean the grout with a bleach-based product, like ✶Scrubbing Bubbles or ✶Comet Soft Cleanser Cream with Bleach and a grout brush. Then apply a grout colorant, like ✶Tile Guard Grout Coating, and afterward use a small brush to apply a coating of ✶Tile Guard Silicone Sealer or masonry sealer. The grout will look like new and resist mildew staining. Reapply in a year. Sealing the grout is the key.

Don't you hate it when someone tells you the same story twice?

• If you ever replace the tile, use colored grout, the thinnest grout line, and the largest tiles (so there will be less grout to clean). You won't have to worry about staining.

• When you buy a product to clean existing colored grout, be sure to read the label and follow instructions carefully.

The floor is hairier than your husband's head

• Every bathroom should have a hand vacuum to pick up hairs quickly.

• If you don't have a hand vac, a great way to wipe up bits of hair is with a nylon stocking.

• ✳ Swiffer Cloths for dusting are great, too. I am not a big fan of using Swiffer Mops for a thorough dusting and washing, but the cloths alone are great for fast clean-ups. Hair sticks to them like a magnet. The key is to keep the mop near the bathroom, so it's ready to go. I don't replace the cloth until I've used it a few times.

Washcloths are all over the place

• Since I use a fresh washcloth twice a day, I put a plastic bin under my sink to collect the used ones.

The soap dish is a mess

• Pop it in the tub while you're taking a bath.

• Or do without one. Instead, use liquid soap on the counter and body wash in the tub or shower.

There are always mountains of towels in the hamper

• Get rid of the towels and supply each family member with a color-coded terry robe that you launder once weekly. Get hooded robes and cut down on hair-drying towels, too.

Your toilet is as dirty as the ones in roadside gas stations

• Drain the toilet by pouring a bucket of water into it. Then use a powerful cleaner that contains hydrochloric acid, like ✶Santeen Toilet Bowl Cleaner. Follow directions on the bottle. ✶The Works make a heavy duty toilet bowl cleaner, too.

• Or use a pumice scouring stick, available at hardware stores.

• You can keep your toilet clean and flushing properly by installing ✶FlushN' Sparkle, a toilet bowl system that sends the cleaner into the

Don't you hate it when someone has used the last piece on a roll of toilet paper?

bowl through the overflow pipe. Since no chemicals enter the tank, the toilet parts won't be damaged.

The toilet tank is scary-looking on the inside

•Keep your toilet tank clean and the bowl won't get as rusty. Pour 1/4 cup of ✳Iron Out into the tank and let it set until the tank is clean before flushing.

Medicine cabinets are stained with rust

• Use a soap-filled steel wool pad or a commercial rust-removing product.

• Line shelves with contact paper to make cleaning easy in the future.

• New medicine cabinets are often rust-proof or rust-resistant. Don't buy one with sliding doors. They're a bear to clean.

Mirrors fog up

• Aiming the blow dryer at the mirror will defog it quickly.

• Or if you're planning to install a new mirror, look for ones that promise to eliminate the fog.

Don't you hate it when you have to hold your glasses together with a safety pin?

Chapter 2
The Bedroom

Don't you hate it when...

You have to wrestle with the duvet cover to get it on

• The easiest way: Turn the cover inside out and lay it on top of the comforter. Grab the bottom corners of both at once, and pull the comforter through.

Duvet corners won't stay in place

• Use binder clips or decorative hair clips at the corners. But if you find these uncomfortable or unattractive, purchase padded ✳Comforter Clips.

You're fighting for your share of the blanket

• Turn the comforter around so the long way is across the bed instead of up and down.

• Or use two comforters.

Don't you hate it when you lose another pair of reading glasses?

There's no place to store the coverlet on warm nights

• Attach a pretty curtain rod or towel bar to the back of your bedroom door.

You don't have space to store blankets and pillows

• I'm sure you've seen the infomercial for the vacuum bags that help store bulky items. (When I tried them, the air leaked out. Maybe they have gotten better.) To make your own version all you need is a heavy-duty plastic bag and a shop vac. Stuff the bag with your blankets and pillows and use the vac to suck out as much air as possible, then tie the bag very tightly.

• Or put the blankets in zippered pillow covers and use as throw pillows.

• Or lay them between the mattress and the box spring.

It's a struggle to pull on the fitted sheet

• The correct way to put on a fitted sheet is to slip on two corners that are diagonally opposite one another, then slip on the other two.

Don't you hate it when you wake up with a painful leg cramp?

• Beware: Many new mattresses are thicker than the older ones and your old fitted sheets might not fit. Look for sheets that have the extra space needed for new mattresses.

You can't remember to turn the mattress

• To remember the jobs that should be done twice or four times a year or so—turning the mattress, cleaning the ceiling fan, checking the batteries in the smoke alarms—time them to coordinate with the change of clocks or the change of seasons: June 21, September 21, etc.

• If you can't remember which side of a mattress should be up next, use a laundry-marking pen to mark a number 1 at the head of one side, then a 2 at its foot, then a 3 at the head and a 4 at the foot of the other side.

The mattress is sliding

• Put a piece of sheet foam at each corner.

• Or lay a blanket between the springs and the mattress.

• Or use a box spring cover or fitted flannel sheet over the box spring.

Don't you hate it when someone describes his dream, in detail?

The mattress pad care label says, "Wash in cold water only."

• That makes absolutely no sense. I've even seen pads that say, "Don't use bleach or hot water." Then how do you get the pad clean and kill dust mites? The wash water has to be 140 degrees or higher to kill dust mites. And it's true, hot water shrinks the pad and repeated washing in bleach will destroy the elastic that holds the pad in place. So what do you do? I use either cold water and 1/2 cup bleach or warm water and 1/2 cup concentrated ✷Lysol disinfectant.

Comforter needs a washing

• I know that some manufacturers say these need professional cleaning, but I've been washing them at home on gentle for years. But you need a large-capacity machine or you may rip the comforter. If your machine isn't big enough, go to a laundromat.

• Use a low-sudsing detergent such as ✷Ivory Snow, because too much soap removes the oil from down. You may need to keep the comforter in the dryer a long time. Be careful: the dryers in commercial places get very hot and comforters should be dried at a medium temperature.

Don't you hate it when a car alarm goes off?

13

Don't you hate it when you replace something you've lost and then you find it?

The mattress is stained

• My favorite device for cleaning a mattress is ✳Bissell's Little Green Machine, the water extraction cleaner used to remove stains from carpeting and rugs.

Your spouse snores

• Most of the many products for this problem have been rip-offs, but if the commercial nose strips are working in your house, see if a bandage will do the job just as well. If so, you'll save a few bucks.

• Ask your spouse to spray a squirt of olive oil into his throat at bedtime. By lubricating the area at the back of the throat, it works as well as many expensive stop-snoring sprays.

• If nothing works and you've tried every earplug on the market, here's another thought: Silly Putty, the kid's clay. Make small balls the size of a nickel and press over the openings of your ears. It worked for me!

Chapter 3
The Car

Don't You Hate It When...

Bugs are stuck on the car bumpers and grill

• Spray with ✳WD-40 and scrub with a soft bristle vegetable brush or a non-abrasive sponge like the ✳Dobie pad.

There are minor scratches on the finish

• Apply a wax crayon that matches the car finish, then buff. The scratches will disappear and the wax will protect the finish and help prevent rusting.

Chrome trim has rust spots

• Use a non-abrasive ✳Dobie pad and ✳Barkeeper's Friend cleanser and polish.

• Use crumpled aluminum foil or #0000 steel wool to rub the spot. Then wipe it with a soft cloth.

• If the surface is rough and dull, apply rubbing compound (available from auto supply departments) with a clean, soft cloth.

Don't you hate it when someone steals the parking space?

You can't remove the bumper sticker

• To remove the bumper sticker that displays the sentiments of your car's previous owner, heat it with a hair dryer until it feels warm, and then carefully scrape it away with a plastic razor blade. (You can get one at an auto parts store.) Or use a credit card for this purpose.

• To remove any leftover glue on the bumper use ✱un-du Adhesive Remover.

You can't get car dealer window stickers off

• If the dealer sticker won't budge, and it's applied with double-sided tape, try this trick using fishing line or dental floss. Hold it tightly and run it under the sticker, using a sawing motion while pulling the line through the adhesive until the sticker falls off. Spray any leftover adhesive with a household lubricant such as ✱WD-40 or ✱un-du Adhesive Remover.

Gunk is trapped in the car's interior cracks and crevices

• Dig it out with a cotton swab, soft toothbrush or mini paintbrush.

Don't you hate it when you have to keep asking somebody to repeat an address again…and again?

• Blast it with a can of compressed air—the same stuff that's meant to clean between computer keys.

There's junk under the seats

• Clean it out fast with a leaf blower. We refer to our leaf blower as Mary Ellen's Dust Buster.

The glove compartment keeps dropping open

• Attach self-stick Velcro strips where the door and interior meet.

Car wipers freeze up overnight

• Buy rug remnants at a carpet or home store and place them under the windshield wipers on cold winter nights. The wipers won't be stuck to the windshield in the morning.

Windshield is covered with film

• Baking soda on a ✱Dobie pad will remove the film without scratching the windshield.

Don't you hate it when a really bad song gets stuck in your head?

Whitewalls aren't white

• Spray on a foaming bathroom cleaner, let it set for 30 seconds, then scrub with a brush and rinse with clean water.

• Or apply undiluted liquid laundry detergent with bleach, scrubbing with a stiff scrub brush.

• Need even more cleaning power? Wet the whitewall with water and then spray on oven cleaner. Leave for ten or fifteen minutes, scrub with a brush, then rinse.

The door lock freezes over

• Dip your key in rubbing alcohol to loosen the frozen lock.

• Or heat the key with a match or the car's cigarette lighter before inserting the key.

• Or use your own warm breath. This works best when you use a straw.

The sun is blinding when you drive

• If the visor doesn't work, stick a large Post-it note on the spot that's causing the glare.

Don't you hate it when the slow driver gets in the fast lane?

Car seats get scalding hot

• If you carry an umbrella in the car, put it over the steering wheel or car seat when parked to keep the surface cool.

• A towel would do the job, too.

The cell phone runs out of juice on the road

• Keep the ✳Emergency Sidewinder Cell Phone Charger handy. It's a light, wind-up generator that provides unlimited emergency power.

Don't you hate it when you're with a friend who can eat just one cookie?

Chapter 4
Carpet & Rugs

Don't You Hate It When...

The carpet gives you shocks

• Spray carpet with water and a dash of fabric softener in a spray bottle.

• Or rub it with a fabric softener sheet.

• Or use a humidifier to add some moisture to the room.

Don't you hate it when you go to a party on the wrong day?

Candle wax drips on the carpet

• Put a plain unprinted brown grocery bag or a plain white paper towel on the spot, and then run a warm iron over it. As soon as the paper absorbs the wax, move a fresh spot of paper where the drip is, and iron again. Repeat until all the wax is absorbed. Make sure you use a bag with no print or you'll transfer the name of the store to the carpet.

A glass of red wine spills

• Immediately blot up as much as you can, using clean white towels. (Do not rub. That will only spread the stain.) Then pour on a bit of white wine. Watch the red wine stain disappear!

Then use another clean white towel to blot up the white wine. Finally flush with club soda or water and blot again. Then cover the spot with another clean white towel and place a heavy book on top of it. When the towel becomes damp, replace it with a dry one.

• Don't have white wine? Then substitute club soda and proceed as above.

Cherry Kool-Aid spills

• My best advice is never to serve cherry Kool-Aid unless you have red carpet. However, if you're hearing this suggestion when it's already too late, a good stain remover to use is ✳Red Erase Stain Remover.

The stain comes back

• That's because the dissolved soil and the cleaning product you used have gotten together and hatched an escape plan. They've wicked back up to the surface as the carpet dried. Apply more cleaner, then lay several sheets of paper towel on the area and put a heavy object, like a book, on top. Leave it for a few hours or overnight and the residue will be absorbed. (Follow this procedure after an initial cleaning and the stain won't return.)

Don't you hate it when you tell people your real age and no one seems surprised?

You can't get the carpet really clean

• Rent a water extraction carpet cleaner. Instead of the cleaner that come with the machine, use 1 T. of powdered ✳Tide detergent per gallon of hot water. For lighter-colored carpets, use ✳Tide with Bleach. (The bleaching agent is hydrogen peroxide, which won't remove color like chlorine bleach.) Just make sure you use a defoamer and rinse thoroughly. (The defoamer can be purchased when you rent the carpet cleaner.) It'll eliminate excess suds, which can be messy; what's more, the more soap you use the more dirt you'll have to clean.

• If you like the smell of pine, add a few drops of pine cleaner or your favorite essential oil.

A braided rug is coming apart

• Don't bother to sew it back together. Use clear fabric glue. If the rug is too heavy to move when you're applying the glue, be sure the floor underneath it is protected. Also make sure the rug is completely dry before you lay it back down or walk on it.

Don't you hate it when a person says, "You remind me of someone" and that someone is not that good looking?

There's a loophole in your warranty

• A friend bought expensive carpeting because it came with a ten-year warranty. When it was stained, she tried to scrub it clean. The stain didn't budge, so she called the manufacturer, expecting the carpeting would be replaced. "Did you scrub?" she was asked. "Yes," she answered. She was told that by scrubbing rather than blotting, she had violated the terms of the warranty. No new rug for her. The lesson: Read your warranty. And buyers, beware.

Heavy furniture leaves dents

• Drop an ice cube on the spot. Let it melt, and then blot up excess water and the dent will pop up. Blot to dry.

• Or use a fork to puff up the spot, and then vacuum over it a few times.

• Or hold a coin on its side and scrape it against the flattened pile.

• Or place a damp clean white cloth over the dents and run an iron over the cloth. The steam will lift the indentations.

• Or use a clothes steamer and brush the dents out with a soft clean brush.

Don't you hate it when people ask you if something's wrong and you're acting normal?

The rug fringe is fraying

• For a good temporary fix, use duct tape to secure the fringe to the underside of the rug.

• Or trim the fringe, if it's long enough. This is especially helpful with bathroom rugs.

The rug fringe is thinning

• Many carpet stores will replace worn fringe on area rugs.

The rug fringe is tangling

• If it's cotton, launder the rug, use a spaghetti-serving fork as a "comb" then spray the fringe with fabric sizing (available alongside spray starch at the supermarket). The fringe stays put and goes back into place if you shake it from time to time.

Don't you hate it when you can't remember whether you've seen the video before?

The rug fringe is more trouble than it's worth

• Just get rid of it. Ask the dealer to remove it when it's purchased.

• Ask a high-quality carpeting store to recommend a dry cleaner that will remove fringe from a rug you already own.

Chapter 5
Cleaning

Don't You Hate It When...

Baseboards are dirty and scratched

• If you don't want to get out the canister vacuum, wear an old pair of thick socks when you're using the upright vac. You can simply wipe your feet across the baseboard, and then use the machine to pick up the leftover dust.

• Dust with a feather or lambswool duster.

• Cover scratches on baseboards with ✳Old English Scratch Remover.

Don't you hate it when you ruin something new while you're trying to get it out of the package?

It's time to clean the basement or the attic

• Before you try normal dusting and vacuuming, get out the leaf blower. It can dislodge the dust and cobwebs from walls and ceilings. When you're opening a vacation house that has been closed for a long time, do the same.

Blinds need to be washed

• Lay towels on the floor below the window. Take down the blinds and lay them flat on the towels, and use all-purpose spray to loosen the dirt.

Wipe away the loosened dirt with a damp towel, and use another clean towel to dry them off. Turn the blinds over and repeat this procedure, rehang immediately. What's most important: Have plenty of clean towels so you're not just moving the dirt around.

• Or install hooks in the shower or somewhere outdoors that can hold the blinds while you wash them down.

• Or bring heavily soiled blinds to a do-it-yourself car wash that has hooks on the wall where you can hang them. Clean off dirt and grime by using the high pressure hoses that shoot hot water. Rinse and wipe or air dry while they hang (so tapes don't shrink.)

Fabric blinds need cleaning

• Check with the manufacturer to make sure fabric blinds are washable. If so, here's a tip I learned from someone who worked in a fabric blind factory. Submerge the blind in a bathtub with warm water and a few squirts of ✳Dawn dishwashing liquid. Let set a few minutes, then pull it out, and continue to dip it in and out of the water until the dirt appears to be removed. Drain tub and fill with clean warm water and rinse. Repeat procedure as necessary. Install hooks to dry in the shower or outdoors.

Don't you hate it when the appliance fixes itself just as the repairman knocks on your door.

• Note: Keep blinds up more than down and they won't get as dirty.

Nothing cleans brick or stone

• For interior and exterior stone and brick, use ✳Klenztone Cleaner. The same formula is used commercially to clean buildings and monuments without sandblasting or acids.

The ceiling is stained with water spots

• Mix equal parts ammonia and water, spray lightly, let dry. The spot will disappear over several applications. This is effective even for a roof leak that causes a yellow stain on the white ceiling. Before you work, put down a drop cloth to protect floors and furniture, and be careful not to get the mixture on wallpaper. Wear old clothes, too; they may get stained.

• To deal with a textured ceiling, mix equal parts of water and bleach in a spray bottle and lightly mist the ceiling. In this case, too, put down a drop cloth, be careful around wallpaper, and wear old clothes.

Don't you hate it when you figure out an easier way after you're already done?

A ceiling is vaulted and dusty

• Use a telescoping tool or just attach a feather duster on a broom handle or PVC pipe with duct tape.

Old cement turns dark

• Apply ✳Klenztone No. 5 to restore it to its white appearance.

Chandelier has lost its sparkle

• Hang an opened umbrella upside down from the chandelier or cover what's below with towels. Spray the chandelier with a commercial chandelier cleaner (following the directions on the can) or mix 3 parts water to 1 part rubbing alcohol in a spray bottle. Let the spray drip off with the dirt. Air dry.

Cobwebs are hanging from the ceiling

• Lambswool dusters on an extension tool are perfect for removing cobwebs in high places. (If yours can't be machine-washed, wash it by hand, roll it in a heavy towel to absorb most of the moisture, then let it air dry.)

Don't you hate it when the person blowing out the candles spits all over the cake?

• Or use an insect-eliminating spray (available near pest sprays in hardware stores). Make sure you purchase a brand that is safe for indoor use. The sprays are usually effective for weeks.

• Cobwebs can indicate an opening where a spider can get in. Maybe it's time to get out the caulking gun.

The driveway pavement is dirty

• A fast food restaurant owner told me that he cleans the drive-thru lane pavement with powdered ✳Tide detergent. Sprinkle it on the driveway, moisten the detergent with water, let it set for an hour or two, then scrub with a long handled brush and rinse off with a hose.

There's an oil stain on the driveway

• Pour cat litter or a scoop of powdered ✳Tide detergent onto a fresh oil stain. Once the oil is soaked up, sweep. Finally, scrub any remaining stain with a paste of powdered ✳Tide detergent and hot water. A 10-pound bag of cat litter will absorb about a gallon of oil.

• For a tough stain, apply ✳Lestoil full strength. Let stand for 15 minutes, then scrub with a wet, stiff brush.

Don't you hate it when you hide something someplace and can't remember where?

Silk flowers are dirty

• Place them in a clean pillowcase. Tie with a knot at the top, place the pillowcase into the clothes dryer with a damp washcloth, set dryer to fluff or air dry for 20 minutes. Flowers come out dust-free.

• Or purchase ✳Pokon Silk and Dried Flower Cleaner. It's the greatest. Just spray it on and dust and dirt vanish like magic. You don't even have to wipe.

Floors don't get clean and shiny

• Whatever they tell you, plain water or water with vinegar won't clean polyurethane floors thoroughly. But I found gentle products that will clean and finish floors and leave absolutely no residue. They were originally called Maid's Choice, and my readers loved them, but they were discontinued. I'm happy to report that I have obtained the formulas and am now selling these products as ✳Mary Ellen's Choice Floor Cleaner and ✳Mary Ellen's Choice Floor Finish. Folks just love the gorgeous "wet" look they produce. They can be used on finished wood floors, tile, quarry tile, marble, slate, terrazzo and vinyl floors.

Don't you hate it when you put cleaning fluids in an unmarked bottle and forget what it is?

It's time to dust or wash the floors

• Have you noticed that Swiffers pads pick up dirt only around their edges? And that no matter how dirty the floor is, they always pick up the same amount? I prefer a dust mop with a large, long mop head that can be laundered. Check the ✶Fuller Brush catalog or call a janitorial supply house and ask them for commercial dust mops. Don't get one too big unless you live in a mansion.

• ✶Sh-mops, which are mops with a washable terry cloth head (you toss in the wash,) are the greatest for washing floors. You can wash and reuse them—and they're so easy to use.

Don't you hate it when you can't look up the correct spelling for a word because you don't know how to spell it?

You can't get underneath the furniture to dust

• To clean under a chest of drawers, simply pull out the bottom drawer to get access for the vacuum.

• Blow dust from under heavy objects such as beds, sofas, refrigerators and so forth with the leaf blower. Do this before you dust the rest of the room.

Knickknacks are coated with grime

• Put small items (including chandelier pendants) in a colander or French-fry basket, submerge them in soapy water, then pull up the colander and rinse the items under very hot water. Let them air dry.

• Or wash them in the dishwasher. Make sure they are secured in place, and turn the machine to gentle wash and air dry.

• Take a good look at your knickknacks. Decide whether or not you really like them or you are spending time cleaning them just because they're there. Remember: Don't clean anything you don't like.

Pleated lamp shades need cleaning

• Use a clean paintbrush to dust between the pleats.

• For sturdy shades use a whisk broom.

• Or blast the dust out with a can of compressed air.

Don't you hate it when your friend brings a surprise guest or two to your dinner party?

All the lamps need dusting

• A ✳dry sponge removes dust and pet hair from lampshades faster than vacuuming with the brush attachment.

• If the shade is attracting a lot of dust, rub it gently with a fabric softener sheet to remove static electricity.

Louver doors are thick with dust

• Use ✳Swiffer Dusters. (Don't confuse these with Swiffer Cloths.) The duster gets in between the slats easily and traps the dust effortlessly.

Stuffed toys are soiled

• Plush nylon toys or those marked "all-new materials" may be washed on cold/gentle with detergent containing fabric softener. Rinse on gentle, air dry for one or two cycles and leave out overnight if further drying is necessary.

• If toys have hair, cover them with a net, cheesecloth or stocking and tie it closed before placing the item in the machine.

• Don't use harsh cleaners or foam rug cleaner on stuffed toys that belong to children still young enough to put them in their mouths.

Don't you hate it when salespeople hover only when you don't want help?

• For a stubborn stain on an unwashable item: Beat one quart of warm water with two or more tablespoons of dish soap until it foams. Then beat the foam only (without dipping beaters below foam level) until it's the consistency of meringue. Dip a dry brush into the foam and spot clean the item, a small spot at a time. Blot off excess moisture with a clean, dry towel. Air dry for 1-2 days, then "fluff" with a dry hairbrush, brushing first in one direction, then the other.

• Unwashable toys may be put in a clothes dryer on "fluff" or "air only." (Prepare for machine handling as above).

You keep running over the vacuum cord

• Vacuum into a room instead of going out of it. The problem won't occur.

The plug pulls out of the outlet while you're vacuuming

• Use a 50-foot extension cord on the vacuum cleaner and you'll save a lot of steps. (Tie the two cords together before plugging them into each other. They won't pull apart. In fact, the harder you pull, the tighter your connection.)

5   Cleaning

Don't you hate it when you don't notice the stain on your shirt until after you've left the house?

You run out of clean vacuum bags

• Here's an emergency solution: Just cut off the bottom of the old one and empty it. Then fold and staple the bag closed.

You can see the handwriting on the wall

• Crayola advises spraying washable wallpaper with *WD-40, then wiping with a soft cloth. Remove any residue with liquid dishwashing soap and water, working in a circular motion.

• *Mr. Clean Magic Eraser does the job too.

A painted wall is dirty

• Why would anyone waste time cleaning a dirty wall when it would probably take less time to paint. Just be sure to vacuum the wall before you paint in order to remove all the dust. Use the bare floor cleaner attachment for the job.

• When you repaint, look for one of the newest formulas, since they can take a lot of scrubbing.

• If you prefer to wash rather than paint, clean the wall with a sponge mop. There's no climbing up and down a ladder, and the job gets done quickly.

Don't you hate it when the waitress brings you coffee that's cold?

• For more stubborn stains and spots, use
✶Mr. Clean Magic Eraser.

It's time to clean windows

• I know the following looks complicated and
long, but trust me; it's the easiest, fastest way to
clean lots of windows. I tried all the hints and
nothing works as well as this. (If you have only a
very few windows to clean see the last bullet.)

– First, remove spots (from tree sap, hard water
or bird droppings). Wet them with water and
scrape with a safety razor. Keep the surface
continually wet to avoid scratching and hold the
razor at a slant.

– Supplies you'll need: ✶Ettore squeegees in the
sizes that fit your windows; ✶Ettore window
scrubber, a cloth-like applicator with a squeegee-
type handle; terry towels; lemon-scented
dishwashing soap (the acid in the lemon helps
cut through the grime, plus it smells clean); and
a three-compartment cleaning caddy with a
handle, the type used to carry and store cleaning
supplies. Two compartments hold supplies, and
the long narrow compartment holds the cleaning
solution. The towel hangs around your neck.

1. Put 2-3 inches of hot water into the long,
narrow section of the caddy. Squirt 3 long

5   Cleaning

**Don't you hate it when
unexpected guests
ask to use the
bathroom and you're
not sure if it's
presentable?**

squirts (about 10 inches) of dishwashing soap into the water and mix.

2. Dip the scrubber in the solution. Apply the thick, sudsy solution to the window. You will have enough solution on the scrubber to apply to several windows without redipping it.

3. Using a dry squeegee blade, take a horizontal swipe across the top of the window. With the towel, dry the uppermost part of the pane so no water is dripping down.

4. Then, putting the blade on a dry part of the glass, begin cleaning the window vertically. Always dry the blade in-between swipes.

5. If there is streaking, let the glass air dry, before wiping off with a dry towel.

6. Be sure to wipe the base and the sides of the window with a towel.

•To clean a few windows only: Spray them with a window cleaner (I like ✳Sprayway Glass Cleaner,) rub with a damp cloth, spray again, then follow the above steps from 3 to 6.

Don't you hate it when the driver coming toward you doesn't dim his bright lights?

Window screens never get clean

• Clean them without water. Use a dry sponge or a vacuum cleaner.

• Or fill a child's plastic wading pool with water (use hot water, if possible) and add dish soap. Scrub each side, using a soft nylon brush with a handle or a paint spreader (a gadget with fuzzy material that you can find in paintbrush and roller departments). Rinse with a hose and dry with cloths or a leaf blower before hanging.

• For metal screens: Spray on foaming bathroom cleaner, leave it on for 10 minutes, gently scrub, then rinse with a hose or shower.

• A viewer told me she took her very, very dirty screens to a do-it-yourself car wash that has hooks on the wall where you can hang them. Shoot streams of hot, soapy water with high-pressure hoses.

Don't you hate it when the elastic breaks on your underwear?

Cleaning products don't work

• You might not be giving the product enough time to show its muscle. Don't just spray and wipe off. Let the cleaning solution stay on the area for 10 minutes, or even longer, so it can do its work. Do something else while you're waiting.

Cleaning products aren't handy

• Store cleaners and tools on each floor of your house and you'll save a lot time running around looking for them. And instead of a cleaning caddy (which takes up too much room) or an apron with pockets filled with bottles and tools (who wants to carry around any weight more than what's actually attached to you?), use a plastic bucket. If I need a bucket, there is always one handy.

Don't you hate it when you tell a friend you're going to stay home, and then run into her when you go out?

The cleaning closet is so full the door won't close

• Most of us have a hard time tossing cleaning products. (Who knows, you might need that bottle of Aunt Bee's Super-Duper Cleans Everything Cleaner someday.) A lot of stuff in there is probably useless, some because it's been sitting around so long that it won't work, and some are brands you don't like or a product you have no need for. Toss any bottles and cans you haven't used in the last six months. If you can't decide what to keep, move everything into another, temporary location, even a carton in a closet. As you need and use it, return each bottle to its usual storage area. Whatever's left in the carton after 4 or 5 months, toss.

Chapter 6
Clothing & Jewelry

Don't You Hate It When...

Your belt isn't big enough

• Use a drill to punch an extra hole. Or have the shoemaker do it.

• If that's not possible, remove the buckle, then sew a two-inch length of elastic (same width as the belt) to the end of the belt and back around the center of the buckle. When the belt is properly buckled, the elastic won't show.

Jeans are too tight

• A tight pair of jeans can be stretched by slipping a wet pair over the bottom of a clean trash can or a cylinder-shaped wastebasket. Don't remove them until they're completely dry.

The loop that holds the belt in place is gone

• To prevent the end of the belt from flapping, use foam poster tabs that you can get in an office supply store to hold it in place.

• Or use pieces of peel-and-stick Velcro.

Don't you hate it when people make you feel guilty about having a delicious dessert?

You can't get your pants zipped

• If they won't zip, lie on your back so your stomach flattens and see if you can zip them up now. Use needle-nose pliers to grab and pull the zipper up.

The zipper is hard to pull

• Attach a key ring to it.

• Rub it with candle wax. There's a special candle wax sold in fabric notion departments for this purpose.

• Rub it with a lead pencil.

• Use masking tape on both sides of the zipper to protect the fabric and avoid staining, then spray the zipper with ✱WD-40 or a silicone spray.

Don't you hate it when pants don't have any pockets?

The zipper keeps unzipping

• Put a button at the top of the zipper and fasten an elastic loop to the zipper to hook it onto.

• Or if it's possible, sew Velcro dots to corresponding parts of fabric at the site where the unzipping is a problem.

Your jeans look too new

• Saturate an old towel with a half-and-half mix of bleach and water and toss it in the dryer with the jeans. Run on "high" for 15–20 minutes. Or mist with bleach in a spray bottle.

• Or mix a thin paste of automatic dishwasher detergent and water in a plastic bowl, using a wooden spoon. Lay jeans flat on an old plastic sheet, and use a paintbrush to spread the mixture unevenly on them. Do other side of jeans, leave for 3-4 hours, wash as usual and dry.

• Or squirt liquid ✳Cascade dishwasher detergent at random over the jeans, turn shower to hot and spray jeans until the detergent has blended into denim. Let stand for 10-15 minutes, repeat on other side, and then launder as usual.

Pantyhose get a run

• Use ✳Elmer's School Glue Stick to stop runs in your hose.

• Keep pantyhose separated in individual plastic zipper bags. Put all hose with runs in a larger zipper bag and reserve to wear under pants.

Don't you hate it when people leave really long messages on your answering machine or voice mail?

• When one pantyhose leg has a run, cut off that leg at the top. In an emergency, you can wear this one-legged pair of pantyhose with another one-legged pair.

Pulling clothing over your head messes your hairdo

• Keep the do in place by laying a silk scarf over your head and hold the four corners in your mouth, then gently slip the article of clothing over your head.

You get mashed-down "hat hair"

• Before putting on the hat, pull your hair up and fasten it at the crown with a barrette. When you remove your hat, take out the barrette, lean over and shake your mane for a just-blown lift.

A purse keeps slipping off your shoulder

• Replace the strap with one that's long enough to wear diagonally across your chest.

• Attach a piece of foam rubber or moleskin to the underside of the strap.

• Keep the purse in place on your coat by sewing a button on the shoulder that prevents it

Don't you hate it when you visit a rest room so fancy you can't figure out how to flush?

from slipping. (Don't sew the button down so tightly that the purse strap will slip right over it.)

Hats lose their shape

• A baseball cap visor will hold its shape if you push it into a tall drinking glass.

• A beret will hold its shape after it's been washed if a dinner plate is placed inside it and it's left to dry thoroughly.

The wind blows your hat off

• It won't happen if you sew two small hair combs into the hatband on each side of the hat.

• Or sew a strip of Velcro inside the crown.

A shirt label is irritating the back of your neck

• Don't cut out the label: You'll just end up with a raw edge that'll be even more annoying. Instead, cover the label with iron-on bonding tape. It holds the label in place and any care or sizing information will remain visible. This works if embroidery inside clothing is scratchy, too.

• Here's a new twist: Tee shirts with no labels. Better late than never.

Don't you hate it when you lose the receipt before you bring an item back?

Your shirt comes untucked or feels uncomfortable

• Trim away as much of the shirt bottom as necessary to make it straight across, then turn up a hem just wide enough to thread a half-inch piece of elastic through it. It looks tucked in and feels wonderful.

Shirtsleeves keep sliding down

• Make a pair of comfortable sleeve garters by sewing together pieces of elastic. Measure your arm so they're not too loose or tight.

• Or use Scrunchies (meant to hold ponytails).

• Or cut strips off the top of a crew sock and slip them onto your arm over your shirtsleeves. Push them up for the perfect arm garter.

Cuffs of the shirt are too large

• Move the button over for a snug fit.

Your sweater has a hole in it

• Stop a small hole from getting bigger by dabbing a dab of clear nail polish or glue on the reverse side of the fabric. It will hold even if the sweater is washed.

Don't you hate it when the special product you purchased to solve the problem, doesn't?

• Your dry cleaner may be able to reweave it.

• Or look up "sweater reweaving" in the Yellow Pages or online at knitalteration.com.

Sweater cuffs are stretched out

• Weave elastic through the cuffs.

• Or sew elastic around the inside of the cuffs.

The sweater has a snag

• Never cut or pull a loose thread. Pull it through to the inside of the sweater with a pin or crochet hook. If possible, knot the snag, then secure the knot with a dab of clear nail polish.

The sweater is pilling

• Use an electric shaver (non-rotary) to shave off the pills.

• Or use a product called ✳Sweater Stone.

• Pilling is caused when a garment rubs against other items during machine washing and drying. So before you launder products that might pill, turn them inside out.

Don't you hate it when the cell phone ringing in the theatre turns out to be yours?

A blouse is gaping open

- Use double-sided tape between buttons.

- For a permanent repair, use Velcro.

- Try a different bra.

Your bra straps are falling down

- Get three safety pins and two rubber bands, and pin one rubber band to each bra strap and fasten it to the center of the bra.

- Check the notions department for (or make a homemade version of) an item that consists of a bit of ribbon that slips around the strap and is pinned to the underside of the garment at your shoulder.

You can't close the button

- Loop a rubber band through the buttonhole and secure both ends around the shank of the button thread for a bit of stretch.

- Preventive measure: When replacing buttons, always use elastic thread for a little extra give. (Alternative: Skip desserts.)

Don't you hate it when the clothing label says pre-shrunk, and it shrinks anyway?

The button won't easily slip through the buttonhole.

• Take a paper clip, and pull it apart so that it's in an S shape. Slip one end through the buttonhole, hook it onto the button, and pull the button through the hole.

Button threads are fraying

• Dab the top of the button with a dot of clear nail polish. Work it into the thread with the nail polish brush. Let it dry and trim any loose threads.

• Or purchase ✴Thread Heaven at a fabric store.

Don't you hate it when you lose a glove?

A button is loose

• For a temporary fix, twist ties do a great job, especially with loosely knit sweaters. Push the wire through the buttonhole and twist it closed on the inside.

• For a quick fix, secure the button with a pierced earring and backing.

A button falls off

• If the button has four holes, sew through two holes at a time, cutting the thread and knotting it for each pair of holes. If one set breaks, the other side will hold.

• Dental floss is much stronger than thread and is perfect for sewing buttons.

• Position a toothpick or match between the button and the fabric when you sew the button, and slip it out when you're done. This is to ensure that you leave enough space for the fabric to slip between the button and buttonhole.

• If you lose a button from the middle of a shirt, you can replace it with the last button at the bottom of the shirt, but only if you tuck the shirt in. Now, you won't have to replace all the buttons.

The drawstring won't stay in place

• Sew a medium-size button on each end of the drawstring and it won't slip through the channel.

• Or tie a knot or double knot close to the end of the drawstring. Make sure it is large enough to stop the drawstring from being pulled out while the garment is in the washing machine.

• To restring a drawstring that has pulled loose, attach it to a safety pin, and wiggle it through.

Don't you hate it when someone borrows your car but doesn't refill the gas tank?

• Take a couple of stitches through the back of the garment to hold the drawstring in place.

The men in your house reveal "plumbers' butt"

• ✶Duluth Trading Company makes extra-long T-shirts for men.

There's a hole in your pocket

• For a temporary fix, try duct tape. But it will get gooey in the wash.

• Notions stores sell replacement pockets. If you can't sew them in, a tailor will.

Your hem is falling down

• Nothing beats duct tape for a temporary hem.

• Fabric stores have clear adhesive tape meant for such an emergency. It's also good for sealing a rip or holding a strap in place.

• ✶Elmer's Glue Stick works, too.

• So do staples!

Don't you hate it when a woman wears knee-high socks with a skirt?

Items slip off wire hangers

• Wind rubber bands around each end of the hanger before slipping the garment onto it. The rubber catches the fabric and keeps it in place.

Pulling on boots is a struggle

• Spray the inside with silicone spray and they'll slip right on.

• Or sprinkle some baby powder inside the boots.

• Or slip a produce bag from the supermarket over your socks. Your feet will slide in and out easily and the bag adds a layer of waterproofing.

New shoes are too tight

• Before wearing the shoes out of the house, slip on thick wool socks and walk around in them for a day or two.

• Or saturate the pressure point from the inside with a cotton ball moistened with rubbing alcohol, then slip the shoe back on. It will stretch as you wear it.

• You'll be more likely to get a good fit if you shop for shoes in the afternoon, since feet tend

Don't you hate it when you still have to tip the hairdresser though you look worse afterward?

to swell later in the day, and you'll be likely to buy a bigger size.

White leather shoes are dirty

• Put a few dabs of a creamy abrasive bathroom cleaner on a soft damp cloth and wipe the shoes clean. Wipe off with another clean damp cloth. Polish as usual.

• Or remove marks with white toothpaste and a damp cloth.

• Or eliminate scuff marks with a slightly damp cotton ball and baking soda.

• Whitewall tire cleaner and white ice skate cleaner from the sporting goods store are both effective on white leather shoes, too.

Don't you hate it when clothes seem to get smaller while they hang in your closet?

Velcro closure won't hold on athletic shoes

• Comb through the Velcro loops with a fine-tooth metal flea comb from the pet store.

Shoelaces fray

• Dip frayed shoelaces into colorless nail polish and form the frayed end of the lace into a point. Let them dry before lacing them.

There's a knot in the shoelace

• To loosen a difficult knot in a shoelace, sprinkle it with baby powder and use the tines of a fork to undo the knot.

Shoelaces come undone

• Keep loose shoelaces tied tighter by spraying them with hairspray before you tie them.

• Or dampen them first. As they dry, they'll stay tightly knotted.

• Look for elasticized laces that convert your tie shoes into slip-on shoes so you don't have to tie them each time.

You step on a wad of gum

Don't you hate it when the top fits nicely but the bottom doesn't?

• Spray it with ✷WD-40; scrape it off with a credit card or dull knife.

White tennis shoes are soiled

• Rinse them off with water, make a paste of powdered ✷Tide with Bleach and spread it over the shoes. Let it set for five minutes before washing the shoes in the machine on a gentle cycle with cool water. Add fabric softener to the rinse water and dry on the line.

Rope-trimmed canvas shoes need a good cleaning

• Brush them with ✻Woolite Upholstery Cleaner.

• Once they're clean, spray with fabric protector to keep them looking good.

Suede shoes are soiled

• Clean with an upholstery cleaner such as ✻Woolite Heavy Traffic Carpet Cleaner, let stand for ten minutes, brush with a ✻Dobie pad or a soft toothbrush and air dry.

• To remove spots and scuff marks, use a very fine grade of sandpaper.

• Try a commercial suede cleaner.

• Ask a shoe repairman if re-dyeing is possible.

Don't you hate it when a "new and improved" product isn't as good as the old one?

Shoes are shabby but you don't have shoe polish

• Wipe shoes clean with a baby wipe, or spray with ✻WD-40 and buff.

• Polish with furniture polish.

• Or use leather wipes made for car upholstery.

Shoes have an odor

• Place them in a plastic bag and set in the freezer overnight. Freezing kills bacteria.

• Fill two old knee-high stockings with cat box filler and tie them shut. Place one in each shoe overnight to absorb moisture and odors.

• Shove a fabric softener sheet in each shoe and leave overnight.

Jewelry irritates your skin

• Paint the surface that touches your skin with clear nail polish.

• Or put a moleskin pad underneath it.

You've lost the earring back

• A pencil eraser makes a temporary substitute. Cut off a small piece from the pencil and pierce it with the post end of the earring.

Your earrings are disorganized

• For clip-earrings, hang a cake cooling rack on a nail or pegboard inside the closet. Hang the earrings on the rungs.

Don't you hate it when you're the one that has to tell somebody about the big crumb that's on their face?

• Push pierced earrings into a piece of needlepoint canvas or a length of fabric held in an embroidery hoop.

All your jewelry's in a jumble

• Line a large, shallow drawer with a textured, light-colored carpet remnant. Beads, chains, brooches, even rings will stay in place.

A bracelet is hard to put on

• Tape one end of the bracelet to your wrist. Clasping it will be a lot easier.

Don't you hate it when the price sticker on the package covers up the moldy strawberries?

Chapter 7
Fix-Its

Don't You Hate It When...

A dripping faucet keeps you awake all night

• Tie a string to the faucet so the water will silently run down it.

The screw won't hold

• Insert a short piece of plastic-covered electrical wire into the hole. (It should be almost as long as the screw). Then reinsert the screw.

• Or cover the screw with aluminum foil and reinsert it into the hole.

• Or take a tiny piece of cotton and soak it with nail polish, poke it into the hole, and replace the screw.

• Or put a bit of steel wool into the hole, then reinsert the screw.

A rusted screw is stuck in place

• Spray it with ✳WD-40.

• If it still doesn't come out, heat it with a hair dryer, and then try again.

Don't you hate it when you've set the alarm for 7:00 pm instead of 7:00 am?

• There are tools such as ✳Xtraktor (a bit that fits into a variable-speed screwdriver) that are meant to solve this problem.

Painting small knobs, bolts or screws is tedious

• Cut X's in a piece of corrugated cardboard and push the items through it; then spray paint them all at once.

You smash your finger pounding in a nail

• Hold the nail between the teeth of a comb to save your fingers.

• Fold a piece of paper and poke the nail through the paper.

Spray painting indoors makes a mess

• Make a paint box to confine the paint mist. Before you start, find the appropriate size carton (anything from a pizza box to a large appliance carton) and put the article inside. Now get out your spray can.

7   Fix-Its

Don't you hate it when your lunch date orders more than you and wants to split the bill?

Paint cans rust

• Transfer unused paint into a thoroughly clean liquid laundry detergent jug so you won't have this problem. Paint will be easier to shake and pour, too. Paint a swatch of color on the front; and remove the label from the can and glue it to the jug.

• Some paint can now be purchased in plastic jugs. The small extra cost is worth it.

You miss spots when you paint the ceiling

• Pick up ✳Ace's Simply Magic Ceiling Paint. It goes on light blue, so you can see where you've painted, but it dries white.

The paint dries out before you're done with the job

• If you cover the roller tray and roller with aluminum foil, or put it in a trash bag (making sure the bag is tightly closed), the paint won't dry out for many hours.

• Use a shower cap to cover paint that you won't be using again for a few days.

Don't you hate it when all the other lines are moving faster than yours?

• Put the paint, covered, in the refrigerator and it won't dry out.

There are dings on the woodwork and walls

• If you store leftover paint in small containers (like baby jars), a quick touch-up is easy.

• ✷Qwikie, a small plastic container that combines a lid and a built-in brush, lets you do a touch-up in seconds.

Wallpaper is peeling up at the seams

• Lift the edge and squirt white glue underneath. Press and wipe away excess glue. Using a seam roller from the paint store, roll the area flat.

You run out of wallpaper border before you finish the job

• A friend purchased wallpaper border on closeout, and just as she was at the end of the job, she realized she was four inches short. Fortunately, she hadn't pasted everything into place. She had a section left to bring to the quick copy shop, where she used a color copier to produce enough of the pattern to finish the job.

Don't you hate it when your pen runs out of ink when you're writing down a phone number?

The wallpaper seams don't quite meet together

• Fill the space with chalk the same color as the wallpaper. The gap won't be noticeable.

• Or mix acrylic paint to match the wallpaper and apply with a tiny artist's brush.

You need saw horses and haven't any

• Two 32-gallon trash containers without lids are great makeshift sawhorses.

You have to dispose of sharp or hazardous items

• Recycle large coffee cans as a receptacle for razor blades and other sharp objects. Make a slit in the plastic lid to push them through.

• Or put tape on the edge of a razor blade before disposing of it.

The plastic top to your glue bottle is gone

• Use a rubber pencil eraser as a cap.

• Sometimes a pen cap fits, too.

Don't you hate it when the preview gives away the plot of the whole movie?

The drawer pull keeps coming loose or unscrewed

• Fill the hole with a bit of steel wool, a matchbook or a couple of toothpicks, and then push the pull into place.

The pictures are crooked

• Use a glue gun to apply a dab of glue on the bottom corners of the frame. Let the glue dry before hanging. The little "mounds" will press against the wall and keep the picture from moving.

• Or place a small amount of mounting putty (available at hardware stores) behind one corner of the frame.

• Or place a piece of folded masking tape (sticky side up) on the bottom two corners of the picture. Stick thumbtacks through the masking tape. The tacks will prevent the frame from shifting.

You're not sure how to hang a picture

• The simplest and most effective way is to use a ✳Heavy Duty Wall Hanger. One end has a

Don't you hate it when you find out the pizza delivery is faster than the ambulance service?

sharp point; push and twist the hanger into the wall until only the hook is exposed.

You put the picture nail in the wrong place

• Insert a thumbtack through a piece of duct tape, then tape it to the back of the frame (with the point sticking out), as close as possible to the middle. Hold the picture against the wall in its desired location and press lightly. The thumbtack will leave a mark where the nail should go.

The wrench is too big to tighten the bolt

• Place a coin between the bolt and the wrench, and then tighten.

You can't tell what's inside a storage box

• Use plastic boxes to keep everything visible and protected from dampness. Buy them inexpensively at discount stores.

• Or, take a photograph of the contents and tape the photo to the outside of the box.

Don't you hate it when people insist on taking candid photographs?

A shelf has warped

• Turn the shelf upside down, place a wrung-out wet towel on the warped spot, put heavy books (protected by waxed paper or plastic) on top and leave it overnight to straighten out.

Spray cans get clogged

• A beauty parlor operator told me she puts the stem in a bottle of rubbing alcohol, sets it back in place, then gives it a few squirts, and it opens right up. She also saves the tip from empty cans to replace clogged tips as necessary.

• After using the can, hold it upside down and spray into a paper bag until the nozzle empties: It won't clog again.

You can't tell where the roll of tape starts

• Before you store the tape, fold the end back on itself so the tape can't stick to the roll.

A door is sticking

• Rub chalk on the edge of the door and then shut it. Open the door and plane the area where the chalk is missing.

Don't you hate it when you write down a really great idea and later on you can't read it?

• Or, if the door is sticking on a high spot, just tape a piece of rough sandpaper underneath. In a few days, normal usage will have done the sanding for you.

Shop vacuum tips over and hoses pull out

• Because canisters are top heavy, they tip over. Also, the hose often separates from the canister when you pull the vacuum during use. Tie a rope around the middle of the hose and attach the other end of it to the nearest wheel on the canister. It's less likely to tip over; and pulling the vacuum from the base rather than the hose makes it easier to maneuver and reduces the chance the hose will pull out.

• Or use a pipe strap and an eyebolt around the hose and another eyebolt near the bottom of the vacuum. Use spring clips to attach the chain to the eyebolts.

Wires, cords and cables are tangled

• Tape them together with duct tape.

• Or use Velcro straps.

• Or cut a length of PVC piping, make a slit in the side, and thread the cords through the slit.

Don't you hate it when you don't have enough arms to carry all of your things?

The light bulb broke off in the socket

• First unplug the lamp or turn off the power. If the bulb is only partially broken, place a thick sock over it and gently tap until the remainder breaks. Place a bar of soap into the broken base, turn, and then twist the bulb out.

• Or do the same with half a potato.

• Moisture can cause outdoor light bulbs to stick when you need to remove them. To ensure that they will unscrew easily, rub a light coat of petroleum jelly on the threads of the bulbs.

Phone buttons stick

• A squirt of ✶WD-40 will do the trick.

Candle wax sticks to candle holders

• Put the candlestick in the freezer and the wax will pop right off.

The ceiling fan is wobbling

• Tape a coin to the top of one of the blades. You might have to move the coin around to different blades until the wobbling problem is solved.

Don't you hate it when the new appliance breaks the day after you've thrown away the carton?

Don't you hate it when the radio station signal comes in clear only when you have your hand on it?

• Or purchase a fan weight in the lighting department of a home store.

There's not enough storage space in the attic, garage and basement

• ✳Stud Buddy has shelves, hangers, hooks and storage bins that are designed to help you use additional space between the exposed studs that may be in your garage and attic.

Glue doesn't work

• ✳Perfect Glue is a three-glue kit that can solve 99 percent of all household glue problems.

• ✳Mr. Sticky's Underwater Glue does the impossible—such as allow you to glue tile back into a swimming pool that's full of water. The product works even when the conditions are wet or cold.

You've stuck your fingers together with superglue

• If you work with superglue, you should know about superglue remover. Buy it at hardware stores and beauty supply outlets (as a remover for fake-nail glue). Follow the directions and product warnings.

A chair wobbles

• Determine which leg is short by setting the chair on a level surface. If the chair has gliders, remove one and place a cardboard washer between the glide and the shorter leg to lengthen it. Replace the glider and check to see if the wobble has been corrected.

• If the chair has no gliders, determine which leg is too long and sand it down to eliminate the wobble.

• Or use wood putty on a short leg. Follow the directions on the can.

Heavy furniture is hard to move

• Slip a skateboard underneath it.

• Or slip an old towel underneath it and pull. That should do the trick, even on carpet.

• Or use waxed beverage cartons or paper plates underneath. It'll glide like an Olympic skater.

• If it's very heavy, use a car jack, and put an old piece of rug underneath it.

Don't you hate it when someone gives you a gift you hate and you have to put it out on display?

White wicker is nicked

• Cover bangs and bruises with Liquid Paper from the office supply store.

The VCR or clock keeps blinking 12:00...12:00...12:00...

• The genius solution: Take a strip of black electrical tape and tape over it.

A really stinky job is facing you

• Mix a drop of your favorite essential oil with a glob of petroleum jelly. Rub it on the top of your lip or right under your nose before you begin. The smell will block out any unpleasant odor.

• Or use Vicks Vapor Rub. Of course this only works if you like the smell of Vicks. I do. It reminds me of my mother taking care of me as a child when I had a cold.

Don't you hate it when beautiful furniture is covered in plastic?

You can't remember how to put back together what you have taken apart

• Before you take it apart, snap a photograph with an instant camera.

Chapter 8
The Kitchen

Don't You Hate It When...

Peeling onions makes you cry

• Wear safety glasses or a swimming mask.

Garlic is hard to peel

• Zap garlic cloves in the microwave for 15 seconds and the skins slip right off.

• Hit the bulb with a hard object, and separate the cloves. Hit again, then remove skins.

• For large amounts of garlic: Press down on the bulbs, remove as much of the papery skin as possible, then place in an electric mixer bowl with the paddle attachment. Mix on low speed until the cloves separate and the peels are removed. The job will be even be easier if you oil the mixing bowl lightly.

There are a lot of salad greens to clean

• To dry them fast, drop clean wet greens into a net laundry bag and tie it shut. Put the bag in a washing machine and set it on spin-dry.

Don't you hate it when you're not sure how to interpret the expiration date on the package?

You don't have a big enough pot to cook all the corn, potatoes, or other vegetables

• Turn your dishwasher into a big pot. When there are no dishes in it, cook as much husked corn as you like. Run an entire cycle (without soap, of course). You might want to do a test run with just a few ears just to make sure your dishwasher doesn't overcook them.

You have to wash bushels of produce from the garden

• Clean it quickly by putting it in the washing machine with two tablespoons of castile soap or ✳Shaklee's Basic H or other mild soaps and running it through a gentle cycle. (But don't try this with very soft items, like tomatoes.)

You need to butter corn on the cob for a crowd

• Pour melted butter into the ditch of a new paint roller pan and roll the corn into it.

• Or spin each cob on a stick of butter.

• Or butter a slice of bread liberally, and spin the cob on the bread.

Don't you hate it when the only ice trays in the freezer are empty?

• For a picnic, fill a mayonnaise jar half full with hot water. Pour a stick of melted butter into the jar. The butter will rise to the top. Dip a cob into the jar. As you lift it out, the butter will coat the cob.

Hard-boiled eggs stick to the shell

• If you cook them correctly, they'll peel easily. Cover the eggs with hot water and bring them to a boil. Cover the pot, remove it from heat, and let eggs set for 20 minutes. Add about one inch of cold water and several ice cubes to the saucepan. Cover the pot and shake vigorously so that the eggs crack all over. Peel under cold running water, starting at the large end.

You have to separate a lot of eggs

• The fastest way is with your well-washed hands. Break the egg into your hand. Spread your fingers slightly and the egg whites will slip between your fingers and the yolk will stay in your hand.

Brown sugar is clumping

• Microwaving will soften it. Zap it in short bursts, or you'll melt it.

Don't you hate it when you can't put things back in the box the way they came?

Avocados and bananas aren't ripe

• Put a hard avocado or a green banana into a plastic bag with an apple. It will ripen within 3 days.

• Or put the avocado in the microwave for 30-45 seconds. Rotate halfway through.

Beets are hard to peel

• Don't peel them, and don't boil them. Just slice off both ends, wrap beet in foil, and bake at 350° for 1 hour. Put on plastic or rubber gloves and peel the cooked beets. The skin will slip off easily.

Squash is hard to cut

• Microwave it for a few minutes before you cut it.

Cheese is hard to shred

• It'll shred more easily in the food processor if you firm it in the freezer for a while.

Cheese is hard to cut

• Heat up a knife and the cheese will be easier to work with.

Don't you hate it when you open a can of soup and the lid falls in?

Crystals form in ice cream

• Prevent crystal formation by storing ice cream in the back of the freezer, away from changing temperatures that come from opening and closing the door.

• Put a piece of plastic wrap on top of ice cream before you close the container and put it back into the refrigerator.

Cooking oil pours out too quickly

• The next time you open a bottle of oil, don't remove the seal. Just cut a slit or poke a hole in it. Then the oil will pour out slowly.

The last drops won't come out of the bottle

• Strap a piece of duct tape onto the side of a bottle, then tape the bottle to the cupboard so it is hanging upside down. Place a bowl directly underneath the hung bottle, remove the bottle cap, and let the remaining liquid drip into the bowl.

• Or do as I do with the catsup: Hold the bottom of the bottle, making sure the cap is on tightly, then spin the bottle around in a circle at your

Don't you hate it when there are more hot dogs than there are hot dog buns?

side (like a Ferris wheel). Centrifugal force will push the catsup to the neck of the bottle.

You can't seal the plastic bread bag tightly

• Clip the bag closed with a clothespin or a binder clip.

• Or grasp the end of the bag, give it a twist at the top of the loaf, then pull the bag back down over the loaf (as if you were pulling a glove inside out, back over your hand).

Soda foams up in the glass

• Rinse the ice cubes with water before putting them into the glass and the soda won't foam up.

You open the soda and it fizzes all over the place

• Before you open the can, tap it on the bottom four or five times.

• Or keep the soda in the refrigerator. Cold soda won't fizz.

Don't you hate it when the smallest size in the coffee shop is medium?

Soda goes flat in the refrigerator

• Tighten the cap of a 2-liter soda bottle, turn it upside down, squeeze a few times, then turn it back up. That reactivates the fizz.

• Mix equal parts of flat soda and fresh and no one will know the difference.

• Or reuse the flat leftovers. Pour them into ice pop molds for the kids or into the ice cube tray to chill a fresh drink.

There's no cap for the soda bottle

• Use a marshmallow.

Don't you hate it when you have to wear an examination robe?

Coffee filters are hard to separate

• Keep a roll of tape with your filters. To separate a single filter from the stack, attach a strip of tape inside it, and then pull.

The stirring spoon slips into the cooking pot

• Attach the stirring spoon to the cooking pot with a clothespin.

The pot burns the food instead of keeping it on simmer

• Make a flame tamer: Cut a large piece of foil and twist it to form a large, thick rope. String it under and over the burner while the burner is cool. When the pot is set on the foiled burner, the food at the bottom won't burn while it simmers for an hour or so.

• Or turn a cast-iron skillet over and place it between the burner and the pot.

• Or place one stove grate on top of another.

A pot boils over

• Prevent boilover by laying a wooden spoon across the top of the pot while it's on the flame.

You have to empty the dishwasher

• To save steps, I set the dinner table with clean dishes from the dishwasher, and then I have only the remainder to put away. I am thinking of installing two dishwashers—one for dirty dishes and the other for clean. I'd hardly ever have to put anything away.

Don't you hate it when green bananas turn brown too quickly?

You can't keep the kitchen sink filled with water

• If water keeps escaping, and you can't leave dishes to soak, put a sheet of plastic wrap over the drain, then push in the stopper.

Drinking glasses are stuck together

• Fill the top glass with cold water and submerge the bottom glass in hot water. Gently pull the top glass off.

You have to hand-dry lots of dishes

• Don't bother. Not only is it more work, it is reportedly less sanitary. (Of course my grandmother towel-dried all our dishes, was never sick, and lived until she was 98.) If you're impatient about letting them air dry, put a fan on the counter.

Don't you hate it when you find out your guest is a vegetarian after you've served them steak?

The liner keeps slipping inside the garbage pail

• Use binder clips from the office supply shop or potato chip clips to hold the bag to the sides of the pail.

Odors linger on your hands

• Hold a stainless steel spoon with all five fingers and run cold water over your hand. Like magic, the odor will be gone.

The counter has a burn mark

• Cover it with a designer tile. Glue it on and use as a permanent hot pad.

Water leaks out when you soak the food processor bowl

• Put an empty film canister upside down over the center spout.

• Cover the bowl with a sheet of plastic wrap before you place the lid on top of it and start the processing. You won't have to bother washing the hard-to-clean lid.

You have to get rid of hot grease

• Pour it into a can, refrigerate it so the grease hardens, then transfer the grease-filled can into a plastic bag (like the one they deliver the newspaper in), and toss it into the trash.

Don't you hate it when you call everyone to the table for dinner and no one budges?

Grease spatters all over the place

• Cover unused burners with a cookie sheet. It's easier to clean a single cookie sheet than several burners and drip pans.

• After you've cleaned the stove, apply *Gel-Gloss to seal and shine the surface. That'll make clean-ups easier.

There's a greasy layer of dirt on top of the fridge or cabinets

• You'll never have to dust if you cover the area with plastic wrap, then replace it occasionally when it's dirty.

• If you install cabinets that go clear up to the ceiling, you'll never have this problem again.

The spatula is too small to flip an omelet or hashbrowns

• Turn a whole panful at once by using a tart or cheesecake pan bottom (without the removable sides) as a huge spatula.

Don't you hate it when you're out of vacuum cleaner bags?

You can't find the corkscrew

• Here's how to improvise one. Insert an eye-screw into the cork. Push a screwdriver through the eye of the screw and pull up to remove the cork.

The jar won't open

• Use a sheet of fine grit sandpaper to hold the jar, grit side down.

• Or use a rubber glove to get a grip.

• Or use the handle of a fork or spoon to pry up the lid slightly, just enough to release the air and pop the button up.

Food is stuck to the pan

• When fried foods like hash browns stick to the bottom of the pan, place the pan in a large pan of cold water. Slide the spatula under the sticky food to loosen it.

• If muffins stick to the pan, place the hot pan on a wet towel and they'll slide right out.

• Spray your grill with the new cooking spray for grilling to avoid sticking.

Don't you hate it when you've asked someone when she is due and she tells you she's not pregnant?

Don't you hate it when you're served a glass of milk and it's lukewarm?

• Spray aluminum foil with cooking spray before cooking and food will not stick.

• Food will not stick to a new pan if you first bring vinegar to a boil in it.

• Fabric softener sheets contain fabric softener and anti-static agents. This combination is great for removing baked-on foods. The anti-static agent weakens the bond between the food and the pan, while the softening agents soften the baked-on food. Just put a fresh fabric softener sheet in the dirty pot, fill it with hot water and let it set overnight.

Peelings and other garbage clutters kitchen counter

• Trap the handles of a plastic trash bag around the corners of a drawer. Hold the side of the bag open and sweep the garbage off the counter into the bag.

• Or hold a tray up to the counter and push the garbage onto the tray.

Drinking glasses are cloudy

• Run the glassware through the dishwasher with detergent and a cup of vinegar.

• If the film doesn't come off with this method, the glasses are permanently etched. Etching may be the result of using too much dishwasher detergent or washing with soft water. Try to use as little detergent as possible; and if you want to use fine crystal, you'll have to hand wash it.

• I have never bought plastic dishware or glasses that didn't etch when washed in the dishwasher, no matter what the manufacturer promised. But if you buy frosted glasses you won't have a problem.

The coating starts to wear off the non-stick pan

• It's easy to ruin nonstick pans with metal utensils and incorrect cleaning solutions. There's a company that will remove existing coating and apply SilverStone to cookware up to 24 inches in diameter at $10 a pan, plus shipping and tax. For information on preparing the cookware for coating contact: OPI Inc. at www.fluorosurfacing.com or at 2208 S. 19th St., Sheboygan, WI 53081-5681, telephone 920-459-5100.

8 The Kitchen

Don't you hate it when the one time you pick up the phone it's the person you've been trying to avoid?

The sterling or silverplate needs polishing again

• Fast remedy: Line a cake pan with aluminum foil and fill with hot water. Add a couple of tablespoons of baking soda and mix thoroughly. Add silver and let set for 5-10 minutes.

• For silver (like candlesticks) that's used only for display, use silver mitts—cloth mittens specially treated to remove tarnish. They're a well-kept secret but they do the job very quickly without any mess.

Burners get spattered with grease

• Cover unused burners with a cookie sheet. It's easier to clean a cookie sheet than burners and drip pans.

The oven floor gets dirty

• Place a sheet of aluminum foil on the oven rack beneath an item whenever you bake to catch spills. To allow proper heat circulation, the sheet should be only slightly larger all around than the pan. (Lining the oven floor with foil may cause heat damage.)

• Also, prevent spills. Don't bake food in containers that are too small.

Don't you hate it when you're daydreaming as the stoplight turns green, and the guy behind you honks?

It's time to clean a dimpled kitchen floor

• Add two tablespoons of automatic dishwasher detergent to a quart of warm water, mop, leave on for 30-45 minutes, wipe clean, then rinse. Since automatic dishwasher detergent has some bleach in it, it may cause color changes, so try this on an inconspicuous spot first. Or use very hot water and a heavy duty cleaner, leave the product on for fifteen minutes, then brush with a stiff-bristled brush to loosen the dirt. Rinse.

Flatware slips down into the garbage disposal

• Buy a drain basket made of wire mesh to cover the drain hole. That lets you safely run the disposal and use your sink at the same time.

Don't you hate it when what everyone else has ordered for dinner looks better than what you've ordered?

Cooking grease covers the walls

• Turn on the ventilating fan whenever you're cooking, not just when there's smoke. It draws up the grease that would otherwise be deposited on the walls and other surfaces throughout the house. It helps get rid of cooking odors, too.

You can't keep track of your favorite recipes

• Write their page numbers on the inside cover of the book.

• Flag them with Post-it notes.

• Or highlight them in the index.

You can't keep the cookbook open to the right page

• Clip the cookbook open with a pant hanger and hang it on a cupboard door.

• A roasting rack will keep the cookbook open.

• Recipes can be slid into Plexiglas frames too.

Don't you hate it when a grocery bag breaks?

Everyone asks, "When are we going to eat?"

• Set the table before you start preparing the meal. A set table signals that a meal is going to be served soon.

Chapter 9
Laundry

Don't You Hate It When...

The washing machine eats the socks

• You (or a handy friend) can pop off the agitator. You may find some hidden there.

• Always put smaller items on the bottom of the wash load. (Small items tend to fall between the tub and the inner works of the washer cabinet and disappear down the drain hose.)

Don't you hate it when you just miss the bus?

Everything is covered with lint

• Don't ever dry lint-creating items such as chenille and new towels with lint-attracting items such as permanent press and corduroys.

• If a pair of pants or other garment is covered with bits of tissue or lint, put it in the dryer with a couple of fabric softener sheets.

A sweater shrinks

• *Cot'N Wash lets you machine-wash and dry cotton sweaters without shrinking, stretching or fading.

A hand-washed sweater takes so long to dry

• An inflatable inner tube placed inside the sweater will speed drying.

• Or make a drying "tool." Put a tee-shirt on a hanger, sew up the bottom and sleeves, and stuff it with plastic packing peanuts. Pull the damp sweater over the drying "tool" and hang to dry. Air circulating though the peanuts will help dry the sweater faster.

• Or fill pantyhose with packing peanuts.

There's a "Dry Clean Only" label on everything

• Manufacturers have to list at least one safe cleaning method on the care label, so many take the least risky path and recommend dry-cleaning. Unless the garment is clearly not washable (wool, satin or something very fancy), you may want to take a chance on washing it in tepid water with gentle soap.

• Despite the label, most sweaters (even cashmere) can be hand washed. In fact, hand washing makes cashmere softer, while repeated

Don't you hate it when you cut your tongue licking an envelope?

trips to the dry cleaner age it. Best technique:

—Hand wash with baby shampoo and cold water, then rinse thoroughly.

—To remove even more water, place the sweater on a large, clean white bath towel, roll it up, and press down on the towel.

—To dry, lay the sweater on top of a dry white towel, on a flat surface, and pat it into its original shape. Never hang it to dry.

Clothes smell musty

Don't you hate it when you can only HEAR the mosquito?

• Toss musty clothing and other items that can't be laundered into the dryer along with a fabric softener sheet and a damp washcloth. Set the dryer on "air," and leave the item inside for just a few minutes. That will freshen the clothes and get rid of any musty odor. The same treatment can be used to deal with items, such as drapes, that have gotten dusty.

• Or use ✶AtmosKlear Odor Eliminator.

Clothes develop mysterious stains in the machine

• Fabric softener sheets can leave greasy marks on synthetics. Wet fabric and rub area with liquid dishwashing soap or ✶Fels Naptha soap.

• Liquid fabric softener can leave blue marks. Rub the spot with ✶Fels Naptha soap or dishwashing soap, or soak the item in undiluted white vinegar until the spots disappear—at least 15 minutes but no more than 30. (And clean the fabric softener dispenser by adding a cup of warm distilled vinegar to the dispenser and leaving it there for an hour or more.)

• Brown spots that appear on your white wash after it goes into the machine mean you probably have a high iron content in your wash water. Add ✶Iron Out along with your laundry detergent.

Stored clothing develops yellow or brown spots

• These occur when whites stored in dark areas are brought into the light or when they are covered with plastic. They may be caused by any of the following: tannin (the substance that makes a cut apple turn brown); brighteners in the fabric that turn yellow in the sun; body oil buildup; bleach the fabric retained in the mill; by iron and manganese in the water. Not all can be successfully treated, but here are some possibilities to try:

• If the spots come from rust (iron and manganese in the water), use ✶Iron Out or

Don't you hate it when your hairdresser finally has it right—and then she can't do it again?

Don't you hate it when you wind up behind the guy with a million packages in the post office line?

another commercial rust remover. For delicate fabrics, use 1/2 t. of ✱Iron Out in 1 c. of hot water. Dip a toothbrush in the cleaner and scrub the spot. Let it soak overnight, then toss it in the washer. Make sure to test for colorfastness first and wash on a gentle cycle.

• On bleachable items, make a paste of fresh lemon juice and salt and apply to the brown spots. Let the item sit outside in the sun for most of the day. Then launder as usual. Or put automatic dishwasher detergent (be sure it doesn't contain ammonia) in a gallon pail, add boiling water until half full, then add 1/4 cup bleach and fill pail with cold water. Add this to wash water.

• Or use ✱Mary Ellen's Formula 1, for colorfast and bleachable items.

You forget to pre-treat stains

• Tie a loose knot in a sleeve or leg or clip a clothespin to a stained area of clothing. When washday rolls around you'll know what garments need special care before you toss them in the washer.

• Keep a stain-removing stick or spray in the bedroom so that when anyone takes off stained clothing, you can pre-treat the spot before you toss the item into the hamper.

Whites get dingy

• ✴Rit Fabric Brightener and Whitener is made to solve this problem.

• Or soak items in your machine for a few hours or overnight in ✴OxiClean, following directions on the container. Add detergent (without bleach) and wash on heavy-duty cycle.

• Or try this classic solution to get whites white again. Add 1 c. liquid bleach and 1 c. automatic dishwasher detergent to your washing machine. Set the machine for a small load and add hot water. Soak overnight, then wash as usual. This is a powerful solution and should only be used when all else fails.

• Or use my personal favorite, which multiplies the cleaning power of bleach many times: my own ✴Mary Ellen's Bleach Booster.

Stains are set in

• Putting a stained item in the dryer is a mistake because once the heat sets the stain it's almost impossible to remove. (But ✴Mary Ellen's Formula 1 for whites and colorfast items

Don't you hate it when you try on sunglasses and that big tag hangs down your nose?

and Formula 2 for colored ones can tackle these problems.)

You don't know how to treat a stain

Here are some stain removal tips that are quick and easy—and they work!

Barbecue sauce

• The owner of a barbecue restaurant shared this idea for removing stains on colorfast bar rags, aprons, slacks and jackets. Stir a cup of automatic dishwashing detergent in a plastic bucket of cold water, add the clothes and soak them an hour or two. Rinse, then machine launder them as usual, using a cold water rinse.

Don't you hate it when you can't quite fit your automobile into the parking space?

Berries

• Stretch the stained area of the fabric taut over a bowl and secure it with a rubber band to hold it in place. Hold a kettle of boiling water about a foot above the bowl. Pour a stream of boiling water right into the stain. The combination of the heat and the pressure works like magic.

• Or rinse the area with cool water. Apply liquid laundry detergent full strength and let set for a few minutes. Rinse and make sure the stain is gone before laundering.

Blood

• For fresh stains, use the trick that nurses use: Pour a bit of 3% hydrogen peroxide on the stain and let it bubble up. Then rinse the spot with cold water. Repeat the process until the stain has mostly faded or disappeared completely, and then launder as usual.

• For difficult and set-in blood stains, I assure you that nothing is as effective as my own ∗Mary Ellen's For Those Days.

Crayon

• Sometimes dipping the clothing in hot water alone will cause the wax to run off.

• If that doesn't do the trick, put item stained side down on white paper towels, apply on ∗Goo Gone, ∗De-Solv-it or ∗Lestoil and let set for a few minutes. Then turn fabric over, spray the other side, and repeat. Launder with ∗Tide with Bleach in the hottest water that's safe for the fabric.

Grass

• First dampen the area, then saturate it with ∗Lestoil or ∗Tide liquid detergent. Let set an hour or so, and launder as usual.

Don't you hate it when the back of your skirt gets caught in the elastic waistband of your pantyhose?

Grease

• To clean up a large grease stain, such as gravy, quickly, cover the spill immediately with cornstarch, which will absorb most of it. That will make it easier to treat the stain with one of the stain removers mentioned below.

• For dirty, greasy work clothes: Treat with ✳Woolite's Power Shot Carpet Cleaner.

• Or use ✳Dawn dishwashing detergent: It's especially good on greasy stains.

• Or wet stain with water and apply ✳Lestoil.

• Or use a degreaser or hand cleaner from an automotive supply store.

Melted gum and lipstick

• ✳De-Solv-It, ✳Goo Gone or ✳Lestoil will remove them all, and clean up the dryer too. Rinse with water.

Ink

• Try ink remover from a stationery store.

• Papermate says that if the item is washable and the ink stained area is small, soak it in warm water with 1 teaspoon ✳Tide, per each quart of water used for 24 hours. For a spot larger than a dime, first soak the item in wood (methyl) alcohol for 15-30 minutes, then launder. (NOTE: This is not safe for rayon, acetate or Celanese.)

Don't you hate it when the elevator door shuts on you?

Paint (latex)

• Flush with running hot water. Now treat with dish soap and water, reapplying and rinsing until the stain is gone. If any remains saturate the stain with ammonia and let it set.

• Oven cleaner removes hardened paint, but use at your own risk and never on wool.

Paint (oil-based)

• ✳De-Solv-It Citrus Solution removes wet oil-based paints and lacquers.

Perspiration/deodorant stains

• On washable colorfast shirts, nothing works better on set-in stains than ✳Mary Ellen's Formula 1.

• ✳Lestoil is good if the stain hasn't been allowed to set in.

• But sometimes what appears to be a "stain" is fabric that has been damaged from perspiration, and unfortunately, nothing can be done.

Soot

• Mix an oven cleaner with equal amounts of water, then soak or spray the sooty items, and launder as usual.

• Or, apply ✳Lestoil full strength.

Don't you hate it when you don't know if you should tell someone his zipper is unzipped?

Tar

• Use ✳De-Solv-It. Follow the directions on the back of the bottle.

Stain removers don't work

• There aren't many stain removers that can remove tough set-in stains, however ✳Mary Ellen's Formula 1 will not disappoint you if you follow directions. It is a miracle product.

Black fabrics fade when washed

• At the last count I had 25 pairs of faded black slacks. It didn't matter if I washed them in cold water and a little detergent, they still faded. Now every time I wash them I add black dye to the rinse water. (Simply dissolve a teaspoon of dye in a cup of boiling water, then add the solution to the cold rinse water.)

• I machine wash with ✳Cot'N Wash. Similar products must be used with cold water to eliminate the fade, but with this one, you can use warm.

• Or use cold water and half the recommended amount of a gentle detergent. Most detergents don't dissolve well in cold water, so dissolve the detergent in hot water before adding it to the washing machine.

Don't you hate it when you figure out what that thingamabob was the day after you threw it out?

Machine drying causes problems

• Fabrics will hold up better if you remove garments from the dryer before they're bone dry.

Clothes are still damp when the dryer goes off

• Dry fewer, larger loads. (Large loads dry better than smaller ones).

• If you only have a few items to dry, drop a large dry towel into the dryer. The towel will absorb moisture and the clothes will dry faster.

• Reset your washing machine for an extra spin cycle when you have a heavy load, and you won't have to keep items in the dryer as long or on as high a temperature.

Items are put in the clothers dryer by mistake

• Put all items that might shrink in the dryer in a large mesh sweater bag before you put them in the washing machine. Instead of sorting through wet clothes, just remove the bag before you transfer everything else into the dryer. Make sure the bag is big enough to hold all the items

Don't you hate it when the finicky eater gets to pick the restaurant?

Don't you hate it when the person with the huge hair-do sits in front of you?

comfortably; if they're crammed together, they won't get thoroughly clean.

You have to iron

• Clothes won't be as wrinkled if you remove them promptly from the dryer.

• Hang garments to dry while they're still slightly damp, and they'll have fewer wrinkles and be easier to iron.

• Your trousers may not need ironing if you hang them by the cuffs the minute you remove them from the dryer. The weight will pull out the wrinkles.

• You'll like ironing better if you use ✷Mary Ellen's Best Press – The Clear Starch Alternative, in the clear bottle. It smells good and doesn't leave any residue.

You don't have an iron when you need one

• Run hot water in a bathtub and hang wrinkled clothing over the steamy tub. Steam relaxes wrinkles and they disappear.

• Instead of steam, use a plant mister on wrinkled clothes. Spritz lightly and leave them on the hanger. Wrinkles may disappear as they dry.

• Ribbons and other small items like a napkin won't need pressing if you just pull them through a curling iron. (Fold the napkins in half first, so they're the right size to pull through.)

The iron shoots out brown water

• Even if you use distilled water, unless you drain an iron after each use, it may leave nasty spots on clothing.

• An iron should be cleaned periodically, too. Here's how: Fill it with white vinegar. Set the iron (soleplate down) on top of a rack inside a broiler pan, and turn it on and let it steam for 15 minutes. Then drain the vinegar, fill the iron with water, and repeat. If the holes stay clogged, use a pipe cleaner to remove the gunk when the iron has cooled.

A shirt is hard to press

• Sprinkle the shirt with warm water and place it in a plastic bag. Microwave it on high for one minute (until it's warm to the touch), and ironing will go much more quickly.

Don't you hate it when your arm isn't quite long enough to reach the itchy spot?

• A long-sleeved shirt won't get all twisted up in the washer and dryer if you button each sleeve to one of the buttons on the shirtfront.

• Spray the collar and cuffs of a shirt with spray starch, and put it on a hanger (preferably one with sloping shoulders, so it won't get the "points" at the end) while it's still damp. The shirt may be worn "as is," especially if it's under a jacket or sweater.

• If you dampen the ironing board instead of the clothing, the ironing will go faster.

The iron soleplate is dragging

• ✴Faultless Hot Iron Cleaner will remove melted webs, fusibles, iron-on interfacings, burned-on synthetics and coatings caused by excess starch and detergent buildup. Irons will glide, which makes ironing easier.

The starch flakes

• You'll prevent flaking if you turn the garment inside out before you spray it with starch.

• Also, let the starch soak into the fabric for a minute before ironing.

Don't you hate it when ironing out wrinkles on one side of the sleeve creates new wrinkles on the other side?

• Best of all: Use ✳Mary Ellen's Best Press –
The Clear Starch Alternative: It's clear, it doesn't
create flakes or leave a residue on dark clothing,
and it's fragrant, too.

You can't get the wrinkles out

• Dip hard-to-iron cottons in a solution of fabric
softener and water and hang them to drip dry.
They're fragrant, and wrinkles fall out.

• To iron clean handkerchiefs, wet them
thoroughly, and then flatten on a smooth surface
to dry.

Jeans don't dry smooth

• Fold wet jeans the instant you take them out
of the washing machine. Lay several pairs or
even a single pair flat when you place them in
the dryer. They will come out just as you
folded them.

• Or just lay them between the mattress and
bed and sleep on the problem. They'll come out
wrinkle-free.

**Don't you hate it when
the top fades and the
bottom doesn't?**

You forget to remove clothes from the dryer

• If they're all wrinkled up, add a damp towel to the load and run it on air dry for another ten minutes.

Plastic or vinyl items (such as tablecloths, ponchos and shower curtains) are wrinkled

• Use a hot iron to heat the ironing board, lay the plastic item on the heated board and smooth out the wrinkles with your hand.

• Or lay a clean pressing cloth (a dish towel is fine) over the wrinkled plastic, and iron on a medium setting.

Tablecloths from the closet need to be ironed again

• Don't iron a clean tablecloth until you're about to use it.

• Or roll tablecloths around cardboard tubes (the long ones, from gift wrap) so they won't crease. Keep them wrong side out so they won't get dust lines or yellow marks.

Don't you hate it when you're the only one who doesn't bring a birthday gift to a "No gifts, please" birthday party?

• Hang tablecloths, napkins or place mats on the back of a closet door with a multi-skirt hanger.

You don't know how to fold the sheets neatly

• Fold a flat sheet in half lengthwise, then halve it again, then do it a third time. Then fold it into thirds to stack neatly. You can tuck the fitted sheet and pillowcases inside it.

• To fold a fitted sheet, slip one corner over each hand, then nestle the two together. Then, slip one doubled set of corners inside the other. Now the sheet is small enough to fold somewhat neatly, and you can tuck it inside the folded flat sheet to keep the linen closet looking orderly.

Towels don't stack nicely

• Lay a towel or washcloth flat, fold it lengthwise into thirds, and then fold that into thirds. (The same method works for pillowcases).

Towels have lost their absorbency

• This happens when fabric softener has been overused. To remove the softener, add 1 c. white vinegar to the laundry rinse water. The vinegar will remove the excess fabric softener.

Don't you hate it when you notice a whiskery hair sticking out of your chin?

You run out of fabric softener

• White vinegar will do the job. Fill your fabric softener dispenser with vinegar or add 1/2 c. to 1 c. to the rinse water. And no, your towels will not smell like pickles. They'll be fresh, soft and sweet-smelling. You may decide to use vinegar all the time.

Sorting clothes takes so much time

• Have a separate laundry basket or cubicle for each family member to stow items as they are folded. Everyone can be responsible for putting his or her own clothes away.

• ✶Sortable Socks have different color-coded logos knit into the bottom of each sock so you can quickly match pairs.

There's no place to store the linens

• Launder the bedding and put it right back on the bed. You save space plus folding time. Make sure you have a spare set of sheets for an emergency.

• Or store sheet sets between the mattress and box spring.

Don't you hate it when you have to play a message over and over because the caller mumbled?

Chapter 10
The Outdoors

Don't you hate it when the nurse says, "Step on the scale"?

Don't You Hate It When...

Cleaning the outdoor furniture takes your leisure time

• Drop the dirty lawn furniture into a swimming pool for eight hours. The chlorine in the pool will clean the furniture and remove mildew stains. (Exception: Don't do this with vinyl furniture.)

• Before a rainstorm, spray plastic resin furniture with a combination of 1/4 c. bleach and 1 qt. of water, with all-purpose cleaner, or with ✳Tilex with Bleach. Let the rain do the rest.

• A pal of mine tosses the furniture (and even the umbrella) in the back of her pickup truck and goes through the car wash.

• Or use the power washer. It's my favorite possession. My power washer does more for me than a diamond ring.

The plastic outdoor furniture is hopelessly dirty

• Paint with ✳Krylon Fusion spray paint. It bonds to plastic without sanding or priming and is available in many colors.

Birdseed grows sprouts under your feeder

• Sterilize your birdseed. Place a gallon of seed in a paper bag and microwave it on high for five minutes.

• Or place it on a baking sheet and bake for 30 minutes at 300 degrees. (Neither method will change the appearance or nutritional value of the seed.)

Lawn chair webbing is ripped

• Use strips of duct tape in place of ripped webbing. Nowadays it comes in many colors, and there's even a transparent version.

Moss grows on the roof

• Sprinkle powdered ✳Tide with Bleach on the roof. Spray lightly with a hose. In a few days the moss will be dead. Rinse it off with a hose or wait for rain to do the job.

The trash cans tip over and spill

• Bungee-cord the garbage cans. First line them up in front of a garage wall or fence. For each can, you need two screw eyes and a 30-inch

Don't you hate it when your arm falls asleep?

Bungee cord. Drill the screw eyes into the wall, attach one end of the cord to a screw eye and wrap it around the garbage can, then attach the other end.

The plastic string breaks on the lawn trimmer

• Coat the line with ✷WD-40 or cooking oil spray.

You have to tip the lawn mower to remove the gasoline

• A turkey baster is the perfect tool to remove leftover gasoline from your lawn mover before storing it for the winter.

• After the last mow of the season, let the mower run until it's out of gas.

Dirt gets tracked indoors when you're doing yard work

• No one will have to take off his or her shoes or worry about the dirt if you place oversized slip-ons at the door. Slide your shoes right inside them as you go in or out the door.

Don't you hate it when you ask somebody if they've seen the latest movie and they tell you the surprise ending?

Your shoes get covered with mud

• Spray ✶WD-40 on your boots before working in a muddy yard. The mud won't stick to them and will rinse off easily.

The knees of your favorite gardening jeans are shot

• Lay them on the table and apply a puddle of clear silicone caulk to each knee. Spread the caulk around with a plastic knife or putty knife until you've covered the whole knee area. Let it dry.

Your arms get beaten up when you cut down shrubs

• Make arm gaiters with a worn pair of crew socks. Cut off the toes, and slip one sock on each arm from the wrist to the elbow. They'll protect your arms and they aren't too hot to wear in the summer sun.

Removing a tree stump will cost a small fortune

• Once you're done grilling, dump hot leftover coals on the center of the stump. Do this as often as you grill. Eventually the stump will be

Don't you hate it when you're having a great dream and you wake up in the middle?

burnt away. CAUTION: Tree roots can burn and start underground fires. Use this tip only when a stump is not surrounded by other trees. Keep an eye on the fire and do this at your own risk.

• Or purchase a stump remover formulation from a garden center.

Plants in clay pots dry out quickly

• Hydrate a clay pot by soaking it in water before you put a new plant in it.

• Paint the inside of the clay pot with marine varnish to prevent it from wicking up water. (Bonus: The varnish will also keep white deposits from forming.)

Don't you hate it when someone tells a very long joke and forgets the punch line?

• Or place a plastic pot inside a terra cotta pot. No more dehydration problem.

Window boxes are constantly in need of watering

• Before you fill the box with potting soil, line the base with several layers of newspaper or a not-too-thick disposable baby diaper (newborn size is ideal). Either will hold onto water so the soil won't dry out as quickly.

Herbicide kills nearby plants

• Weed killers are powerful and can be lethal to plants you want to save. So cut an inch or two off the bottom of a 2-liter soda bottle and set it over the weed. Place the nozzle of the weed killer into the neck of the bottle and spray. The bottle shields surrounding plants. (Weeds with deep root systems need to be killed with a chemical herbicide. If they're pulled by hand, some of the root may remain and the weed will return with a vengeance.)

• Or dip a clean paintbrush into weed killer and carefully brush the weed.

There's no place to put the weeds when you're gardening

• Instead of having to look for a trash can, place large lightweight attractive garden pots or garden hose containers at strategic places around the garden. Toss the weeds in as you work.

• Or carry plastic grocery bags when you're checking out your garden. Toss weeds into it, then throw out the whole thing.

Don't you hate it when they tell you there's only a 30 percent chance of rain and it's raining?

119

Brown patches appear in the lawn

• When dogs or diseases cause spots, instead of planting seed in the summer, make a patch. With a flat spade, cut out the damaged spot (square or rectangular cuts are easier to deal with) and remove it, along with 3 inches of soil. Find a lightly trafficked spot (such as behind the garage), cut out a similarly shaped piece of sod, and transfer it to the prepared hole, watering it well. Keep the patch moist and soon it will blend in seamlessly and in the fall reseed the area where you harvested the patches.

Don't you hate it when you can't remember who borrowed your favorite book?

Garden hoses are a tangled mess

• Keep hoses neat and tidy by storing them in a round laundry basket.

A inexpensive water sprinkler tips over

• To make a budget-priced water sprinkler stay put, pull the hose through a cinderblock brick (with holes in it) and then attach the hose to the sprinkler. Now it'll stay in place while it's in use.

You can't keep the leaf bag open when you're raking leaves

• A 2x3 piece of cardboard placed inside the leaf bag will keep it standing straight. When the bag is half-filled with leaves, remove the cardboard and the bag will stand by itself.

• Use a tall bucket instead of your hands to press the leaves into the bag. You'll pack them more tightly and use fewer bags.

Camping supplies and personal items get wet

• Use a coffee can to store toilet paper, matches, candles, and cameras.

• At the beach, use a coffee can with a lid to protect your camera, wallet, keys, or any other valuables from water and sand.

There's no outdoor sink to wash your dirty hands

• Put a bar of soap into an old nylon stocking and tie it to the outside faucet.

Don't you hate it when you arrive way too early for a party?

Beach sand is in your bathing suit

• Sprinkle baby powder on the sand, then brush off the baby powder along with the sand.

Your tennis balls go onto another court

• Paint a face on each one with a marker and you'll know in a second which of the balls belongs to you.

Napkins fly away at a picnic

• Use a spring clothespin or a supersized binder clip to hold the stack together.

Don't you hate it when your friend thinks it's funny when she lets out one of your secrets in public?

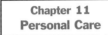

Chapter 11
Personal Care

Don't You Hate It When...

You spray on too much perfume

• Moisten a cotton ball with a little rubbing alcohol and rub it lightly over the area where you've sprayed the perfume.

You run out of makeup remover

• Use a "no tear" baby bath product or baby shampoo. Put a few drops on your fingertips and apply it to your eyelids, then wipe it off with a damp cloth. You may want to use these products on a regular basis. They're much less pricey than products sold specifically for this purpose.

Don't you hate it when someone acts like they know you, but you can't remember who they are?

The manicure doesn't last

• Before you polish, apply a little vinegar to each nail with a cotton ball. The polish will stay on longer.

• Brush baby oil on freshly painted nails to prevent nicks and chips.

Lipstick breaks

• Press the lipstick into a small, empty plastic
container and use a brush to apply it.

The lipstick cap won't stay on

• Wrap electric tape around the base of the
container and the cap should fit snugly
once again.

Lips are dry and flaky

• Smooth them out with any product that
contains salicylic acid, and the lipstick will look
much better.

**Don't you hate it when
people describe their
digestive problems?**

Your favorite makeup is no longer being manufactured

• There are online sources that will match any
shade. (Search "custom blended makeup" or
"custom blended lipstick.")

The bathroom scale isn't accurate

• To reset an adjustable scale, get a couple of
five-pound bags of sugar or flour and place them
in the spots where your feet would be. Turn the

dial until it says ten pounds. Lift the bags and set them down again, until the ten-pound mark stays steady. Then the scale will be in balance. (Don't you also hate it when the scale registers too high and it's right!)?

The curling iron is sticky with hairspray

• Dampen a cotton ball with nail polish remover and run it along the surface of a cool curling iron. Wipe with a damp cloth, dry with a second cloth.

• Remove encrusted mousse and other hair products by spraying a cool iron with oven cleaner. Let it sit briefly, then wipe it clean with damp sponge. Air dry.

Tweezers are losing their grip

• Give them a rub with sandpaper or an emery board.

• For the world's greatest tweezers, check out this site: www.Tweezerman.com. They manufacture items you can't find everywhere, like nose hair trimmers, mini shavers, and a variety of eyelash curlers.

Don't you hate it when you're in the dressing room and you can't figure out how to put the garment on?

Plucking your eyebrows hurts

• Numb the brow area before you tweeze. Use a product meant to soothe teething baby's gums.

Self-tanner causes dark splotches

• Wipe a depilatory over the affected area with a tissue, wait a minute, then rinse off. That should even out color without leaving light spots.

There are yellow stains on your nails

• Soak nails in plain water for a few minutes. Then brush nails with an old toothbrush dipped in a solution of 1 c. water and 4 capfuls of hydrogen peroxide.

Your hair looks dull

• To remove product buildup and give hair shine, add a little baking soda to your shampoo.

Hands feel greasy or sandpapery

• Squirt shaving cream in one hand, sprinkle sugar on the other, rub them together and rinse.

Don't you hate it when the gynecologist says, "Now, just relax"?

• If your hands are dirty from shop work and you don't have granular soap, clean your hands with a mixture of dishwashing soap and sugar.

• To soften your hands, pour a T. of olive oil or baby oil in your palm, rub your hands until they're well covered, then sprinkle on a teaspoon of sugar and do the same. Rinse them off under warm water.

Your feet are dry and rough

• Before taking a long walk, rub your feet with petroleum jelly, and then slip on thick walking socks. When you return, your feet will be as soft as a baby's bottom.

Coffee, tea, and cigarettes stain plastic braces

• A dentist told me to mix soda and hydrogen peroxide to the consistency of yogurt and apply the mixture to my teeth (but not to my gum tissue) with a soft bristled brush. If it burns, dilute the mixture with water. Repeat daily for 10 to 14 days and you should see improvement.

• Or try whitening strips or toothpaste.

Don't you hate it when the nurse asks why you're there within earshot of the whole waiting room?

Braces shine in a photograph

• Rub a bit of petroleum jelly on them (it will refract the light) and rub it off after the photo session. Models use this tip.

You can't see if new glasses look good on you

• Take a Polaroid or digital camera along when you pick out new frames. Have a friend (or the salesperson) snap you in your top choices. You won't have to squint into a mirror to see how the frames look on you.

You have a wart

• Most warts can be removed with an over-the-counter aerosol spray that freezes them. They should fall off in 10 days. If not, try again.

• Or try the method that a dermatologist tipped me off about: He said covering a wart with duct tape for six weeks would make it disappear.

• Or see your dermatologist for treatment with liquid nitrogen.

Don't you hate it when the dentist says, "You won't feel this" and you do?

You get a splinter

• If you put a drop of iodine on the splinter, it'll be easier to spot for removing with tweezers.

• Or put a bit of rubber cement or white glue on the spot, let it dry, and pull it away. It very likely will take the splinter along with it.

• Extracting the splinter will be painless if you first numb the area with ice or a product that soothes a teething baby's gum.

There's no ice pack when you need one

• Wrap a dishcloth around a frozen juice can and you have an emergency ice pack.

• Or use a pack of frozen peas.

Don't you hate it when someone tells you your million-dollar idea has already been done?

**Chapter 12
Pests & Pets**

Don't You Hate It When...

Mosquitoes ruin the fun

• They hate wind, so I blow them off my deck by running a large fan.

Outdoor sprays and lotions are greasy and smelly

• If you can't stand smelly, greasy outdoor lotions and sprays that attract more insects, use ✳Ugly Bugly and always be comfortable in the outdoors. It's safe for the entire family.

Bugs are all over the place

• Use a shop vac to suck up bugs, but make sure there's soapy water in the canister so the bugs don't escape. (Since dead bugs stink, dispose of the bag immediately.)

• ✳Hot Shot Foggers are great to kill bugs that are hiding in basements, attics, garages, pet sleeping areas, and cabins.

Don't you hate it when you can't remember if you're on the lather, rinse, or repeat step?

Wasps are ruining the picnic

• To get rid of wasps and bees, coat a few pieces of cardboard with maple syrup and place them at a distance from the picnic table. The pests will be attracted to the sticky treat and get stuck.

• Or cut off the top of a two-liter bottle, fill it with sugar water, then top it with a funnel that fits over the bottle. The sugar water attracts the wasps and they'll travel through the funnel to get to the water and become trapped.

• Or squirt some dishwashing soap into a half can of Mountain Dew. The sweet soda attracts the pests, so they'll climb into the can for a drink and that's that. Make sure nobody picks up the can and takes a drink or that'll be that.

Don't you hate it when the foil candy wrapper touches your filling?

• Or sprinkle sugar on the sticky side of a sheet of contact paper. Hang to trap wasps.

Ants are congregating

• Buy safe boric acid bait stations from home and hardware stores.

• Or mix 4 T. maple or corn syrup with 1 t. of borax. Poke holes into a jar lid, then place a dab of the ant bait on the inside of the lid.Put the lid on the jar and set it in areas frequented by ants.

The hummingbird feeder is infested with ants

• The simplest and most effective way to get rid of ants in the hummingbird feeder is to use an ant moat (a small cup-like device that hangs between your feeder and your hook).

• There are built-in moats in ✳HummZinger and ✳Hummerfest hummingbird feeders.

• Or wrap flypaper around the hanger between the feeder and the hook.

• Or coat the hanger with petroleum jelly and they'll stay away.

Wasps have joined ants at the hummingbird feeder

• Try moving the feeder a few feet in any direction. Insects are not very smart, and they will assume the food source is gone forever. They may never find it in its new location, while the hummingbirds will barely notice that it was moved.

• If that doesn't work, take the feeder down for a day or until you stop seeing wasps looking for it. Hummingbirds will be looking for it, too, but they won't give up nearly as soon as the wasps.

Don't you hate it when if just a few numbers were different you would have won the lottery?

Cockroaches are a problem

• Years ago I came up with the best way to kill cockroaches: Get them drunk. Put a couple of inches of cheap wine into a large coffee can and place it under the sink. The cockroaches crawl into the can, start drinking, get drunk and drown. For a cockroach, there are worse ways to die.

• Osage oranges (sometimes called hedge apples) are said to repel cockroaches and spiders.

• Try sticky traps from hardware stores. Once you know where the roaches are hanging out, use a shop vac (with soapy water in the tank) or a Hepa-equipped vacuum to suck them up.

Box elder bugs are bothersome

• Vacuum them away. Toss the bag before you bring the vacuum into the house. If you use a shop vac, add soapy water to the tank. Once the bugs are sucked up they'll drown.

• Box elder bugs hang out near and on box elder trees. Get rid of the tree.

A bat's in the house

• Close doors to rooms adjoining the one with the bat, but open doors and windows that lead to

Don't you hate it when you get the answering machine and you know the person you called is at home?

135

the outside. Sit quietly and wait for the bat to fly out. (The lights can be left on.) The bat will follow the air currents and escape.

• If that doesn't work and you're brave, try trapping the bat underneath a large basket or another container, then sliding a piece of stiff cardboard or a thick magazine underneath. Take the "cage" outside and free the bat.

• Or throw a towel or blanket over the bat and take it outside, then let it go.

• When you try to trap the bat, come up from behind so it won't detect your approach.

Flies are swarming

• Hang plastic zipper bags filled with plain water from the eaves. The reflected light may be what turns them off. Start with a few bags, and if the flies are still a problem, add more. (The price is right!)

Grain moths invade the house

• Grain moths can be found in rice, pasta, and cake mixes; rat or mouse bait; breakfast cereals; children's art work (that contains pasta, corn, etc.); herbs and spices; any grain, feed, and seed; and dried vegetables (decorative or edible)

Don't you hate it when the turbulence starts just as you've gotten your meal tray?

or dried fruit. Often they come into the house in birdseed. Don't buy any bag of seed that's sticky. (The stickiness is evidence that pests going in or out of the bag have released the seed's natural oils.)

• When you bring seed home, transfer it to plastic containers, then freeze. Moths will die after five days or so.

• Feed should be stored only in an airtight container. Never bags.

Squirrels take over the bird feeder

• Use a baffle that protects feeders from squirrels. They're sold in bird stores.

• To keep squirrels off the top of a baffle, smear it with a mixture of petroleum jelly and a few drops of hot sauce. The application lasts for months.

Animals rummage through your garbage

• Spray the garbage pails with pine-scented cleaner or insect repellant.

• Or keep dogs from even coming over to your area. On the boundaries of your property, set out one or more gallon-sized cartons (glass or

Don't you hate it when your ears don't pop on the plane?

plastic) filled with water 2/3 of the way up. If that doesn't help, try putting out more containers that are placed closer together.

Your dog is covered with burrs and thorns

• Work a little baby oil into the tangle, and then brush the tangle loose with a brush or a mat-splitter brush. For tougher burrs, carefully crush the burr with a pair of pliers before brushing it out.

• Spray the area with ✴WD-40, then wash it with soap and water.

Don't you hate it when the end of the book is a total letdown?

There are pet hairs everywhere

• Slip on a rubber glove, wet it and slide your hand along the upholstery. Hairs will be attracted to the rubber like a kitten to a ball of yarn.

• Or use a ✴Swiffer Cloth.

• Or use a ✴dry sponge to pick up pet hairs from upholstered furniture.

• Afterward, rub the area with a fabric softener dryer sheet.

• To keep drapes from collecting pet hairs at the bottom, spray the hem area with anti-static spray.

• Get hairs off the carpeting by misting it with diluted liquid fabric softener, let it dry, then vacuum. Damp mop hard surfaces.

Pets go where they don't belong

• Cats will stay away from a furniture leg if you wipe it with chili or Tabasco sauce or with liniment. (Blot all of it thoroughly.) You can't smell it, but the cat can.

• Oil of cloves rubbed onto table legs seems to deter puppies.

• Keep cats out of the planters by putting clothespins in the soil about 6" apart.

• Or cut a hole for the stem of the plant, then cover the soil with a plastic saucer.

• Pinecones or horticultural charcoal will keep the cat's paws away, too.

• Outdoors, put fir boughs around shrubs where cats leave their mark. They like to cover up after themselves, and since boughs will prevent this, they'll stay away. Bonus: this is a non-toxic solution; and the boughs protect plants from winter cold as well.

Don't you hate it when the smoke blows your way?

The dog's dish keeps tipping over

• When your pet is outdoors, use an angel food cake pan with a wood stake through the center as a feeding bowl.

The dog barks non-stop

• Squirt lemon juice in the dog's mouth while ordering him to be quiet. Your dog will definitely get the message.

The pooch rejects the cheaper food

• Fill a spray bottle with chicken broth, spritz the food, and watch his tail start wagging.

Fido meets a skunk

• Mix a quart of 3 percent hydrogen peroxide, 1 c. baking soda and 1 t. liquid soap. Bathe the animal, rubbing the mixture into the fur for about three minutes. Take care to avoid the eyes and rinse well. Repeat if necessary. Just in case you were with Fido, it'll work on you, too.

• The best all-around commercial odor remover in my opinion is ✳AtmosKlear.

Don't you hate it when you tell someone you aren't feeling well and the person complains about feeling worse?

Chapter 13
Various Hassles

Don't You Hate It When...

Pieces are missing from your crystal or china service

• Call (or visit online) ✶Replacements or ✶The China & Crystal Center. They can probably locate any pieces you need, even if your pattern is no longer being made.

Your luggage gets lost

• When flying with your companion, pack half of your clothing in his or her suitcase and vice versa. If one suitcase gets lost, you will both still have things to wear.

The plane arrives late and you miss your connecting flight

• Don't join the crowd around the counter. On your cell phone or from a pay phone, call the 800 number to book another flight and then go to the ticket counter or straight to the gate to do the paperwork.

Don't you hate it when you forget someone's name immediately after you have been introduced?

The airline confiscates your eyebrow tweezers

• ✳Tweezerman makes an airline security carry-on travel kit that adheres to current airline security requirements.

Shipping costs for online shopping are expensive

• When you shop Sears, Borders, Lowe's, Best Buy and other national retailers, you can pick up your purchase at a nearby branch.

Houseplants die when you go on a long vacation

• ✳DriWater tubes will keep plants watered for over 90 days.

The Christmas tree won't stand up straight

• Step on a foot pedal and the ✳Christmas Tree Genie secures trees up to nine feet tall and trunks up to seven inches in diameter.

Don't you hate it when the guy sitting in front of you lowers the back of his airplane seat?

Your address book is a mess

• Write each address on a recipe card and slip it into the plastic sleeve of a 3" x 5" photo album. When a change is needed, toss the old and add the new. (The card can also record birthdays and other information.)

You can't manage all the shopping bags

• On a mall trip, take along a luggage carrier (the foldable type that has an elastic cord to hold the luggage). It handles the bags perfectly.

You're having a snack attack

• The detergent in toothpaste causes sweet and salty foods to taste bitter. When you're craving a bag of cookies, go brush your teeth.

There's gum in your child's hair

• Rub in some peanut butter; you'll get it out.

The warranty expires just before something breaks down

• Try every feature on your appliance before the warranty period ends.

Don't you hate it when the restaurant singers come over to your table to serenade you?

Chapter 14
Products

Product Suggestions

For your quick reference, here is a list of specific products I recommend in this book. Many are widely available, but when I thought a product might be hard to locate, I have listed a specific source. In any case, you can always go to my web page (www.maryellenproducts.com) or call 800-328-6294 if you need more information.

AtmosKlear Odor Eliminator. Superior removal of odors of all kinds. Biodegradable, non-toxic. www.maryellenproducts.com or 800-328-6294.

Band-Aid Water Block plus Finger Wrap. Superior to all similar products. In drug stores.

Barkeeper's Friend. Removes rust and other tough stains on hard surfaces without scratching. At supermarkets in the cleaning section with other cleansers.

Bissell's Little Green Machine. I like the new ProHeat model. Available at home stores and where most vacuums are sold.

Cascade Dishwashing Detergent. At supermarkets.

China & Crystal Center. Replacement china and stemware. 952-474-2144.

Don't you hate it when the cashier has already rung up your huge order when you realize you don't have your wallet?

Christmas Tree Genie Device. Holds the tree straight. www.krinnerusa.com.

Comforter Clips. Holds duvet and its cover together. www.cuddledown.com or 800-323-6793.

Comet Soft Cleanser Cream with Bleach. At supermarkets.

Cot'N Wash. Keeps cotton sweaters from shrinking and fading. www.maryellenproducts.com or 800-328-6294.

Dawn Dishwashing Liquid. Great degreaser. At supermarkets.

Dobie pad. Non-scratching scrubbing tool. At supermarkets.

DriWater Tubes. Keeps plants watered when you're not there. www.driwater.com or 800-255-8458.

dry sponge. A rubbery sponge that removes grime and dirt without water. At home/hardware stores.

Duluth Trading Company. Sells extra-long T-shirts for men. www.duluthtrading.com or 800-505-8888.

Elmer's Glue Stick. For easy, no-mess bonding. In supermarkets and stationery stores.

Don't you hate it when your plane arrives early and there's no open gate so you sit and wait on the runway?

Emergency Sidewinder Portable Cell Phone Charger. Small, powerful, very light, wind-up generator. www.sidewindercharger.com or 406-522-9300.

Ettore Squeegees. Makes window cleaning easy. Available at hardware and home stores.

Faultless Hot Iron Cleaner. Removes buildup on iron soleplate. At home/hardware stores and supermarkets.

Fels Naptha Soap. Stain-removing soap. At supermarkets.

Gel-Gloss One-step Cleaner and Polish. At hardware stores and www.gel-gloss.com

Hair Catching Brush. Removes hair that's clogging drains. www.homesew.com or 800-344-4739.

Heavy Duty Wall Hangers. They require no tools to install and hold up to 100 pounds. www.heavydutywallhanger.com

Hot Shot Indoor Fogger. Clears away pests. At home/hardware stores.

HummZinger and Hummerfest. Hummingbird Feeders. At bird/garden stores or www.birdfeeding.com or 401-247-1854.

Don't you hate it when the vending machine eats your money?

Iron Out. Removes rust from fabrics. In the plumbing department of hardware stores.

Ivory Snow Detergent. At supermarkets.

Klenztone Cleaners. Formulas available to clean different stones, bricks, and more. www.klenztone.com or 800-331-1696.

Knit Alteration. For reweaving sweaters. www.knitalteration.com or 800-662-5648.

Krylon Fusion. Spray paint that adheres to any plastic surface. At home/paint stores or krylon.com.

Lysol Concentrated Disinfectant. At supermarkets.

Lestoil. Concentrated Heavy Duty Cleaner. Removes tough stains. Cleans garage floors and other surfaces where grease and oil exit. At most supermarkets or 800-537-8645.

Mary Ellen's Best Press – The Clear Starch Alternative. A clear and fragrant starch that doesn't clog, flake, or leave any residue on dark fabrics. It (almost) makes ironing fun. www.maryellenproducts.com or 800-328-6294.

Mary Ellen's Bleach Booster. Boosts the power of bleach many times. www.maryellenproducts.com or 800-328-6294.

Don't you hate it when the winner is about to be announced and they go to a commercial?

Mary Ellen's Floor Cleaner and Finish.
You'll love the "wet" look it creates on your floors.
www.maryellenproducts.com or 800-328-6294.

Mary Ellen's Formula 1 (for white, bleachable clothing) and **Mary Ellen's Formula 2** (for colored, washable clothing). My stain removers are powerful enough for even set-in stains.
www.maryellenproducts.com or 800-328-6294.

Mary Ellen's For Those Days. Removes set-in blood stains instantly.
www.maryellenproducts.com or 800-328-6294

Mr. Clean Magic Eraser. Wet the eraser with water, squeeze, then rub stains off most surfaces. At supermarkets.

Don't you hate it when you have to wait until next week to know the ending?

Mr. Sticky's Underwater Glue. Holds under water. www.underwaterglue.com or 916-961-4700.

Old English Scratch Cover. In the cleaning product section of supermarkets.

OxiClean Laundry Detergent. Deep-cleaning action of the stain remover combined with an effective laundry detergent. In supermarkets.

Perfect Glue. A kit with three different glues and a chart that shows you which to use when.
www.perfectglue.com or 866-321-GLUE.

Pokon Silk and Dried Flower Cleaner.
Available at craft stores and at
www.weddingflowersandmore.com
or 866-588-7455.

Qwikie Paint Touchup Kit. www.qwikie.com
or 866-227-3861.

Replacements, Inc. Replace broken china
in many patterns. www.replacements.com
or 800-737-5223.

Rit Brightener and Whitener. Brightens
dingy clothing. At mass merchandisers or
www.ritdye.com.

Santeen's Toilet Bowl Cleaner. Powerful
formula for toilets that look impossible to clean.
At hardware stores or maryellenproducts.com.

Shaklee's Basic H. Gentle, safe, yet effective
cleaner. www.shakleeproducts.com.

Sh-Mop. The best mop to wash floors.
www.maryellenproducts.com or 800-328-6294.

Scrubbing Bubbles. At supermarkets.

Simply Magic Ceiling Paint. Goes on blue
(so you can see what you missed), dries white.
At Ace Hardware.

**Don't you hate it when
you can't remember
why you came into
the room?**

Sortable Socks. Makes matchup easy.
www.amazingsocks.com or 888-472-5678.

Sprayway Glass Cleaner. My favorite glass
cleaner. At many hardware stores and supermarkets
or www.maryellenproducts.com.

Stud Buddy Storage. System for exposed stud
walls. www.studbuddy.com or 888-578-7452.

Sweater Stone. Removes pills on sweaters.
www.sweaterstone.com or 425-392-2747.

Swiffer Cloths. Great to pick up hair on floor
and for quick cleanups. At supermarkets.

Swiffer Dusters. Tools that get between slats of
louvered doors. At supermarkets.

The Works. Powerful cleaners that are priced
right. At supermarkets.

Thread Heaven Conditioner. Keeps threads
from fraying. At fabric stores and herrschners.com
or 800-441-0838.

Tide Laundry Detergent. This super detergent
does many amazing things. From removing tough
stains on clothing to killing moss on roofs. At
supermarkets.

Tile Guard Grout Coating. Makes white grout
white again. At home/hardware stores.

**Don't you hate it when
someone says the
punchline before you
finish telling the joke?**

Tide with Bleach. At supermarkets.

Tile Guard Silicone Sealer. Seals clean grout. At home/hardware stores.

Tilex with Bleach. Removes mineral deposits, mold, and mildew from tiles. At supermarkets and home stores.

Tweezerman. Useful, hard-to-find items such as nose hair trimmers and mini shavers. www.tweezerman.com.

Ugly Bugly Outdoor Lotion. No harsh ingredients such as DEET, petroleum, animal byproducts, or alcohol. The patented formula was developed by a scientist/missionary in South America. I'm the lucky gal who gets to tell you about it. www.maryellenproducts.com or 800-328-6294.

un-du Adhesive Remover. At hardware and home stores or www.un-du.com or 888-289-8638.

WD-40. Household lubricant and glue remover that has hundreds of uses. At home stores and supermarkets. (Visit www.fanclub@wd40.com.)

Woolite Upholstery Cleaner cleans fabric shoes as well as upholstery. At supermarkets.

Don't you hate it when you get a leg cramp while you're sleeping?

Woolite Heavy Traffic Carpet Cleaner.
Effective on suede shoes as well as carpeting.
At home stores.

**Woolite Power Shot Carpet Stain
Remover.** Not only removes tough stains from
carpets but works great on clothing too. At most
supermarkets.

Xtraktor Screw Remover. Removes damaged
or stripped screws. www.xtraktortools.com
or 866-987-5867.

**Don't you hate it when
you can't find the coat
check stub?**

Trademark Information

"Band-Aid" is a registered trademark of Johnson & Johnson.

"Barkeeper's Friend" is a registered trademark of Servaas Industries.

"Bissell's Little Green Clean Machine", "Little Green" and "ProHeat" are registered trademarks of Bissell Homecare, Inc.

"Cascade" is a registered trademark of Proctor & Gamble, Inc.

"Comet" is a registered trademark of Prestige Brands International.

"Chrome-R-Tile" is a registered trademark of Santeen Products, Inc.

"Cot'N Wash" is a registered trademark of Cot'N Wash International.

"Crayola" is a registered trademark of Binney & Smith, Incorporated.

"Dawn" is a registered trademark of Proctor & Gamble, Incorporated.

"Dobie" is a registered trademark of 3M.

"DustBuster" is a registered trademark of Black & Decker.

"Elmer's Glue Stick" is a registered trademark of Elmer's Products, Inc.

"Ettore" is a registered trademark of Ettore Product Co.

"Faultless Hot Iron Cleaner is a registered trademark of Bon Ami Co.

"Fels Naptha" is a registered trademark of Dial Corp.

"Gel Gloss" is a registered trademark of TR Industries.

"Hanes" is a registered trademark of Sara Lee Corp.

"Hot Shot" Fogger is a registered trademark of Spectrum Brands.

"Iron Out" is a registered trademark of Iron Out Inc.

"Ivory Snow" is a registered trademark of Proctor & Gamble, Inc.

"Klenztone" is a registered trademark of
K & E Chemical Co.

"Kool-Aid" is a registered trademark of Kraft Foods,
Incorporated.

"Krylon" is a registered trademark of the
Sherwin-Williams Co.

"Liquid Paper" is a registered trademark of
Liquid Paper Corp.

"Lestoil" is a registered trademark of The Clorox Co.

"Lysol" is a registered trademark of Reckitt Benckiser.

"Mountain Dew" is a registered trademark of
Pepsico, Incorporated.

"Mr. Clean" Magic Eraser is a registered trademark
of Proctor & Gamble.

"Old English" Scratch Cover is a registered trademark
of Reckitt Benckiser.

"Original Scrunchie" is a registered trademark of
Scunci Int'l.

"OxiClean" is a registered trademark of Orange Glo
International, Incorporated.

"Papermate" is a registered trademark of Newell.

"Plexiglas" is a registered trademark of
Atofina Chemicals, Inc.

"Polaroid" is a registrated trademark of Polaroid Corp.

"Post-it" is a registered trademark of 3M.

"Red Erase Stain Remover" is a registered trademark
of Evergreen Labs.

"Rit" is a registered trademark of Best Foods.

"Scrubbing Bubbles" is a registered trademark of
S.C. Johnson & Johnson, Inc.

"Shaklee's Basic H" is a registered trademark of
Shaklee Corp.

"Sh-mop" is a registered trademark of Komsentech,
Incorporated.

"Silly Putty" is a registered trademark of
Binney & Smith, Inc.

"SilverStone" is a registered trademark of Dupont Inc.

"Sprayway" Glass Cleaner is a registered trademark of Sprayway, Inc.

"Swiffer" is a registered trademark of Proctor & Gamble.

"Tabasco" is a registered trademark of McIlhenny Co.

"The Works" is a registered trademark of HomeCare Labs.

"Tide" is a registered trademark of Proctor & Gamble, Inc.

"Tile Guard" is a registered trademark of Homax.

"Tilex" with Bleach is a registered trademark of Clorox.

"Velcro" is a registered trademark of Velcro Industries.

"Vicks" & "Vapor Rub" are registered trademarks of Proctor & Gamble.

"WD-40" is a registered trademark of WD-40 Co.

"Wine Away" is a registered trademark of Evergreen Labs.

"Woolite" is a registered trademark of Reckitt Benckiser.

Tell me your favorite Don't You Hate It Whens and send them in! If I use one of your tips on our website or in any of our publications, I'll send you a FREE book. In the event of duplicates, the book will go to the person whose submission I open first.

Mary Ellen

Send your tips to: **Pinkham Publishing**
Attention: Turtle, Box 10, Grand Rapids, Minnesota 55744
Or E-mail me at: m.ellen@bitstream.net